Praise For
~ Turn of Phrase ESL

"Recognizing and using English idioms and phrasal verbs is essential to fluency. My students love learning and using idioms, but we can only cover so many of them in class. This series gives learners a fun, contextual way to access and learn a plethora of idiomatic phrases. I'm so excited to recommend these books to my students!"
~ Brynna Larsen, English as an Additional Language Teacher, Bonn International School

"I'm pleased with the user-friendly model employed—a thoughtful, well-designed, and systematic approach to teaching second language learners important features of English, including but not limited to idiom, figures of speech, authentic English expression and collocations. I look forward to introducing this series to my Chinese undergraduates next semester."
~ Michael D. Brown, Professor, English as a Foreign Language, Nanjing Agricultural University

"A focus on vocabulary, activation of prior knowledge, and the stimulation of higher order thinking are core principles identified by the Center for Applied Linguistics. The TOP ESL books not only support these research-based practices, they promote strong student-to-text interactions in a fun and creative way."
~ Areli Schermerhorn, ESL, World Languages, and Bilingual Peer Observer, Syracuse City School District

"TOP ESL is a great advancement in the education of English language learners. Idioms and colloquial expressions were always the most difficult aspects of language to teach in the ESL classroom. With TOP ESL, students are able to learn the meanings behind common idioms and catchphrases in books with attention-grabbing plot lines. This is the type of resource that would have been greatly valued when I was teaching, and I hope that future ESL students take advantage of what is now at their disposal."
~ David Whalen, Former ESL instructor and Addictions Counselor, Dave Smith Youth Treatment Centre

CLEANING HOUSE

A Chooseable Path Novel for Learning English Expressions

Rebecca M. Karli

Turn of Phrase ESL

Night Owls Press

Cleaning House - A Chooseable Path Novel for Learning English Expressions (Turn of Phrase ESL)
Cleaning House Copyright © October 2015 by Rebecca M. Karli.
Turn of Phrase ESL Copyright © October 2015 by Night Owls Press.
All rights reserved worldwide.

Turn of Phrase ESL
www.nightowlspress.com/turn-of-phrase-esl/

Published by Night Owls Press LLC, Portland, OR, 97203, U.S.A.
www.nightowlspress.com
Designed and printed in the United States of America.

Editors: Genevieve DeGuzman and Karen Hannah
Production Editor: Andrew Tang
Cover artwork by Rick Kitagawa and Eve Skylar

Paperback ISBN-13: 9781937645137
E-book ISBN-13: 9781937645120
Library of Congress Control Number: 2015910701

For my mother who has always believed in me as a writer.

[CONTENTS]

[INTRODUCTION]

WITH MORE THAN a million words, the English language is considered one of the most varied and changeable languages in the world; new words and phrases are always being added. Much of this diversity comes in the form of idiomatic expressions: *Ring a bell. Face the music. All decked out. Bad egg. Down to earth. Train of thought.* You hear these expressions in everyday conversation or read them in books, newspapers, and magazines. Idioms and other forms of expression introduce you to words that have many different meanings and teach natural communication patterns, broadening your understanding and use of English. Learning how to recognize and use these expressions will make you a more confident, fluent English speaker.

Turn of Phrase ESL (TOP ESL) introduces intermediate to advanced level English language learners to idioms, phrasal verbs, and collocations in the form of chooseable path novels. TOP ESL offers you what no other books on the education market can: a rich source of idiomatic expressions; meaningful contexts of those expressions in action; and a gamebook reading format that will have you hooked with cliffhangers and plot twists.

As immersive learning experiences, TOP ESL's gamebooks are effective learning tools. Researchers have long shown that learning a language in meaningful contexts can help students become more fluent and improve retention. The gamebook format provides the contextual literacy that is so important in language education. With their chooseable path structure, the books aren't just an absorbing storytelling experience but are also a fun story*making* one. As you immerse yourself in the stories and lives of the characters in the books, you become fully engaged in your own learning.

How to Read This Book

Gamebooks are fictional narratives told in the second person and interspersed with decision points. Decision points present readers with a choice between several options. How readers choose determines the direction of the story. Following the typical gamebook format, TOP ESL books feature decision points every few pages. Decision points are

How the story unfolds depends on you.

either 'language-based,' testing your understanding of particular idioms, phrasal verbs, and collocations, or 'situational,' testing your understanding of the narrative context—story logic, character motive or behavior, and themes. With more than sixty decision points in each book, TOP ESL offers many opportunities to master new vocabulary and idiomatic expressions and boost reading comprehension and literary appreciation.

But be careful. Sometimes the difference between the options you encounter can be subtle, and sometimes there isn't an obvious right or wrong answer. *A stranger uses a particular expression, so how do you respond? You are faced with a dilemma and must decide between two courses of action, so which one do you take?* The option that best fits the context of the story leads to better outcomes. A good decision may present you with an opportunity or a bit of luck; a not-so-good decision may lead you down a dangerous path. Whatever you decide, your fate rests on the choices you make as a reader.

To enhance your learning experience, relevant idioms, phrasal verbs, and collocations in the text are bolded for easy identification. "Tested" expressions and phrases that appear in the decision points are defined in the Glossary at the back of the book. As a bonus for teachers and students alike, suggested activities and lessons for the classroom and self-study will be made available at www.nightowlspress.com/learning-guide-turn-of-phrase-esl/.

IN *CLEANING HOUSE*, you are faced with a challenging mystery. Your mother has disappeared. Nick, your cousin, says that one of the last things your mother said to him before she vanished was that you could help. But how? You aren't a detective—not a real one anyway. You learn about Cleaning House, Inc., the agency your mother worked for. Going undercover, you find yourself chasing a trail of strange clues. Every day that passes, you get more desperate and afraid. You may not know what you are doing, but you do know you must do everything it takes to find your mother.

There are three individuals who will either help or block your investigation: Nick, your overly confident cousin; Cat, Nick's beautiful girlfriend, who may or may not have good intentions; and Betty, your mother's coworker at Cleaning House, Inc. Listen closely to what they say to you and how they answer your questions. Anyone could be hiding something. Anyone could be lying to you.

And don't worry: If you make a wrong decision, there is usually a way to get back on the best path. Use your English language skills, try your best, and you will solve this mystery and find your mother.

narrative 叙述；故事
Interspersed 点缀的；散置的
idioms 成语；方言
dilemma 困境
outcomes 结局；产出

CLEANING HOUSE

A Chooseable Path Novel for
Learning English Expressions

[CHAPTER ONE]

~ Dirty Laundry

THE CHILL IN the morning air reminds you that summer is almost over. You are enjoying the last few days of vacation at your grandmother's house before returning to the university to start the school year. For weeks, your routine has been the same. You drink your morning coffee on the front porch, and then you **settle in** with your favorite crime novel. These days, **losing yourself** to a good book is your only **guilty pleasure**.

You **take a sip** of coffee and look around you. On the streets, people walk by leisurely, **waving their hellos** to neighbors. *Everything is so … normal and boring.* In your latest novel, the main character is an **undercover agent** who travels around the world on secret missions. You fantasize about being a character in your book.

From inside the house, the phone rings, **breaking your concentration**. Your grandmother **turns down** her radio and **picks up the line**. You close your book and hold the coffee mug in your hands, straining to hear your grandmother's conversation. Her friends call her all the time, and you expect to hear her friendly chatter for the rest of the morning. But after a few more moments of whispering, you realize that something is different.

Your grandmother **calls out**, "David, it's for you. It's Nick."

You almost spill your coffee.

Nick is your cousin. You haven't heard his voice since he moved to Washington, D.C. five years ago. When you were **growing up**, you lived with your mother, grandparents, and several cousins, including Nick. Nick often acted like your big brother, watching over you, especially after your grandfather died. You two were close back then, the only male teenagers in a house full of women. But lately, you have been **out of touch** with your cousin, except on Facebook. It seems **better this way**. After the fight you had with your mother, you have never wanted to talk about anything personal with Nick. You don't want to bring back those **bitter memories**, and you want to keep it that way.

Why is Nick calling me now after all these years?

You run into the tiny kitchen where your grandmother is now busy cooking. "Hello?" you speak into the mouthpiece, your **heart beating** fast.

"Kiddo! How are you?"

You wince at the sound of your childhood nickname. Nick is only a few years older than you but has always insisted on calling you "Kiddo," like you are a child. When you were younger, you hated it; you still hate it now.

"Fine," you answer. "Getting ready for classes. I'm going to medical school next year."

"Yeah, I heard. Congratulations."

"Thanks," you respond. "And you? How's life in D.C.?"

"I'm doing okay. I'm making **good money** in construction. I'm even starting my own window washing service. After all this time **scraping by** and doing **odd jobs**, I think I'm finally doing **something that matters**. Anyway, I've got a new girlfriend . . . "

Nick was always competing with you over girls, money, and popularity. Since you were kids, Nick has wanted to **show you up** at every opportunity, competing for the family's attention—especially your mother's. You wonder if he has news about her. Your stomach tightens. Your mother is the one person you don't ever want to think about. You try to keep the conversation on him.

"A girlfriend? She must be blind if she's **going out** with you," you tease. "What's her name?"

"Cat," he answers, his voice softening. "You'd love her, Kiddo. She's a waitress, but she's trying to become an actress. That's her passion. Anyway, I'm calling now because it's time you come by and visit D.C."

"You're joking, right? I can't believe you're even asking. You know I can't—"

"You can't or you won't? This is about your mother **for crying out loud**."

Nick's outburst surprises you. A long silence **rings in your ear**.

"Look, I know you and Ana aren't **on speaking terms**, but she needs you now."

Yes, you and your mother haven't spoken in years. But it wasn't always like that. You both used to be very close. When she went to the States to work, she became your hero. She sent you money, toys, and clothes. She called every week, and you wrote her letters. She promised you one day that you would be back together. Either she would bring you over, or she would come back home when she saved enough money.

Broken promises . . .

Instead, she bought Nick a plane ticket. Her excuses were **little comfort**. She explained it was because he was older and had the job skills to get work in the city. She wanted you to stay where you had the opportunity to study at a good university. You soon stopped answering her letters and phone calls. Years passed without the two of you speaking to each other. Sadly, it is just how things have **panned out** between you and your mother.

"So," you slowly ask, feeling the burn of **old wounds**, "how is Ana doing these days?"

"Ana?" Nick repeats, with some impatience. "Dude, she's your mother. Anyway, that's exactly why I'm calling." There is panic in his voice now. "I—I don't know how to tell you this. I think something has happened to her."

"What?"

"Ana didn't call me this week like she usually does. It's our routine, so I got worried and tried calling her. I couldn't **reach her**, so I went to her apartment. She wasn't there. The weird thing is that the door was unlocked. I found a plate of food on the dining table untouched and the TV still on."

"Did you try **reaching her** at work?"

"Yeah, I called the cleaning agency where she works. They said she **came in** a few days ago. She **completed her shift** as usual, but she hasn't **reported to work** since."

A sense of dread **fills you**. As part of her job, your mother cleans strangers' homes and offices. It is well-paying, honest work, but it always sounded a little risky to you. Nick usually **makes fun** of you for worrying about her. He always blames your suspicions on your crime novels and your imagination. This time he doesn't mention it.

"There's more," Nick continues. "Just a **little while ago**, I got a phone call from her. She didn't **sound like herself**."

dread 恐惧
suspicion 怀疑

If you decide to respond with, "What do you think was wrong?" go to **page 5**.

If you decide to respond with, "Who did she sound like?" go to **page 7**.

"What do you think was wrong?" you ask. You know something very bad must have happened for her to leave without telling anyone, especially Nick. **As far as you can tell**, the two of them are close. If your mother didn't **sound like herself**, then Nick would know something was wrong.

"I don't know. **Something was up**. She was whispering and talking really fast, so I couldn't hear everything. And I was at work, too. I was distracted. I think she was worried someone was following her or listening to our phone call."

"Hey!" an impatient voice yells in the background on Nick's side. "Is he coming or not?"

You hear Nick cover the phone with his hand, though you still can **make out** his voice. "I'm working on it!" he answers the person.

Then you hear him abruptly **hang up** the phone. He is gone. The **line is dead**.

Standing in front of you, your grandmother covers her mouth with her hand. You **exchange silent looks** of worry. You wrap your arms around her shoulders and lead her to the living room as you explain what happened. "I'll do what I can," you promise, though you are still unsure how you can help.

You try to convince yourself that it might all be a misunderstanding. Maybe your mother needed a vacation and just didn't tell Nick where she was going. Or maybe Nick is just playing one of his jokes on you.

Still . . . what if?

You decide to do something you haven't done in years: You **swallow your pride** and **call back** Nick.

"Sorry about that, Kiddo," he apologizes. "I, uh, had to do something for my boss who can be a pain in the—"

"So what did she say?" you interrupt, trying to bring the conversation back to your mother.

"Who? Your mother or my boss?"

"My mother," you say impatiently.

吕柳柳闪说

"Right, right," Nick mumbles, as if he were **collecting his thoughts**. "Well, it was odd. She mumbled something about revenge for **airing someone's dirty laundry** years ago."

If you think that Nick is saying that your mother revealed someone's secret, go to **page 8**.

If you think that Nick is saying that a client or coworker was unhappy with a job your mother did, go to **page 11**.

"Who did she **sound like**? Are you positive it was my mother?" you ask nervously.

"What?" Nick asks confused. "Of course it was Ana. Do you think she would pretend to call me and act as if she were someone else? Hello! Not your mother's style."

"You said she didn't **sound like herself**, that she was pretending to be someone else," you insist. "Maybe there was a reason she was **disguising her voice**—"

"**There you go again**, Kiddo. I think you're confusing your crime novels for real life."

As you replay Nick's explanation of the phone call from your mother in your mind, you realize that your cousin meant something was wrong when your mother called. She wanted Nick to notice that she was in some kind of trouble.

disguising 伪装
mumble 含糊地说
dread 恐惧
suspicion 怀疑
make out 辨认出
outburst 爆发
tease 取笑
comfort 安慰
wince 抽搐

Go to **page 5**.

Nick is saying that your mother revealed someone's secret. Well, it **makes sense**. A housekeeper could easily **come across** incriminating evidence—**dirty laundry**—while cleaning a person's home or office.

You imagine your mother, a tiny woman in her cleaning uniform, standing in front of a group of reporters, explaining how she helped put a criminal in prison:

*"How did you know the **suspect**?" one reporter would ask.*

Your mother would pause, and then, looking down at her hands, say, "I was his housekeeper."

*Then another reporter would **jam a microphone** in her face. "And where was the suspect hiding the stolen money?"*

Your mother would answer, "I accidentally found it in the suspect's bedroom, hidden in a sock, inside the laundry basket."

You grip the phone. "This is serious then," you say to Nick. "Did she ever talk about anyone? Coworkers? Clients?"

"No, I don't think so," Nick answers.

"The police should be investigating everyone she has ever worked with to **get to the bottom of this**."

"The police don't seem to know anything, or they're not doing enough to find her. They're **looking into** her clients. So far, they don't have any **leads**. She's your mother. I'm afraid this is all **up to you** now." He pauses. "And she did ask for you specifically. I do remember that."

"Really? But why me?"

"Why you? Well, you've always been the smart one," Nick answers with a hint of envy. "I wouldn't even know where to start. Honestly, I'm **clueless**, David. And you're so good at solving mysteries. When we were **growing up**, you used to pretend you were a detective. I never **got away with** anything at home because of you."

Nick is right. As a child, you always loved **solving cases**: a neighbor's missing dog, your grandmother's misplaced eyeglasses, a friend's stolen bike. You smile to yourself as you remember the time you solved "The Case of Grandfather's Missing **Dirty Magazines**." You found them under Nick's bed.

You think about how your mother was a big reason becoming a detective was your childhood dream. When your mother still lived at home, she would always **play along** with you, pretending to be a witness and giving you clues through riddles and secret codes—sometimes even real codes. Your mother's interest in ancient cultures made her familiar with **Mayan hieroglyphs**. The pictograms of animals, people, plants, and the stars were like a **secret language** between the two of you.

"That was a long time ago," you answer quietly. "Playing detective—that was a kid's hobby. I've changed. I'm studying to be an eye doctor for **crying out loud**."

"Eye doctor. **Private I**. Hah—it's perfect," Nick jokes. "Look, Ana's got her reasons. She seems to think you know something or have some way to help her."

Secrets. Scandal. Corruption. Revenge. Did my life just become like one of my books?

Your mother says she needs you. She may have **let you down** by not coming home all these years, but that doesn't mean *you* have to **let her down**. You don't know how you can help, but even if there is just a **small chance** that you can, you should go. You should do the **right thing**.

"Okay, I'll **book my flight** as soon as possible. But just promise me something, Nick. When I get to D.C., don't tell anyone who I am or why I'm there."

"Not even Cat?" Nick **sounds** hurt.

"Not even your girlfriend. I need to keep a **low profile**."

Nick laughs nervously. "Don't worry. I'll tell everyone you're my buddy, Kevin, visiting from **out of town**. Yeah, it sounds like a good **cover** for you."

"And one more thing," you add.

"Yeah?"

"Don't call me Kiddo anymore."

There is a long pause. "I'll call you whatever I want to call you," Nick says gruffly, and then he **hangs up**.

Now, that's the Nick I remember.

Go to **page 12**.

Nick is saying that a client or coworker was unhappy with a job your mother did. She often complained about some of the unpleasant people she worked with. Some of her clients were inconsiderate and demanding, and a few of her coworkers would **take advantage** of her and try to claim responsibility for her work.

You try to remember if there is anyone in particular she would **hold a grudge** against. Would your mother be angry enough to do something to a rude client or coworker—something serious enough to make that person want revenge **in return**? You shake your head. Whatever you feel about her, your mother is still a good person **at heart**.

"My mother has always been professional about the work she's done. Even if her clients or coworkers did sometimes **drive her crazy** with their laundry demands, she wouldn't—"

"No, you don't **get it**," Nick says, **cutting you off**. "This has nothing to do with her cleaning work."

You pause and try to think about what Nick is saying to you. His words make you recall all the crime novels and detective stories you have read **over the years**. *Secrets. Scandal. Corruption. Revenge.*

Then you realize the true meaning of **airing dirty laundry**. It doesn't have anything to do with dirty clothes. Your mother found out about someone and exposed his or her secret. And now that person is **making her pay**.

Go to **page 8**.

A few days later, you **fly out** to Washington D.C. You take a taxi from the airport to Nick's home downtown. It is eleven o'clock at night when you arrive in front of an apartment building on a quiet, tree-lined street.

"Here we are," says the taxi driver.

"Thanks," you say, giving him the fare and opening the car door.

"Maybe you should call first," the driver says, leaning over the seat. "It's late. Make sure everyone is **up**. You don't know how many times people get stranded outside of buildings because the person who was supposed to let them in fell asleep. It happens more often than you think."

"I left my cell phone back at home; besides, it doesn't work here anyway. I also talked to my cousin from a payphone after I **landed**. He should know I'm coming."

"You don't have a working phone?" He is shocked, as if such a thing were possible. You can see his worried expression in the rearview mirror. Then he snaps his fingers. "**Wait a minute**," he says. "I think I have an old phone somewhere. Let me see . . . " He goes through the glove compartment and hands you a nice-looking smartphone.

You can't **believe your luck**. "I can't accept this." You appreciate the man's generosity and kindness, but you would feel bad taking an expensive phone for free. "Let me at least pay you something for it."

"Nonsense. Please take it," he insists. "My daughter got me the new iPhone for my birthday anyway, so I've been looking to **get rid of** this one. It's still prepaid for the month. I'm on another plan with the new phone, so you can have the minutes that are left on there. It has Wi-Fi."

He shows you how to turn it on, and you call your cousin. When Nick answers the phone, he sounds annoyed like you just woke him up, but he says he will come right downstairs. You can hear a woman talking in the background.

"You were right," you admit to the driver.

You thank him again for the phone and go and meet your cousin and Cat in the first floor lobby of the apartment building.

"Hey, Ki—I mean, Kevin," Nick exclaims as he greets you. He gives you a big hug, lifting you off the ground. "Man, look at you," he says, looking you up and down. "Exactly the same. Skinny as ever. You're a toothpick. When are you going to **put some meat on those bones**?"

You feel your face **turn red** when you **make eye contact** with Cat. She is stunning—a tall, **leggy**, beautiful blonde. Standing next to her, Nick is **half a head** shorter though double her size in width. In fact, he looks like a tank. You can see how the muscles in his arms bulge against his clingy shirt. He has obviously been **working out**, probably spending all his **free time** at the gym.

Cat seems to be **studying your face**. "So how do you know Kevin again?" she asks Nick.

"Oh, right," he answers, putting his arm around Cat. "Let me introduce you two. Kevin, this is Catherine Fisher, but I call her Catfish. And Catfish, this is my best friend from when I was a kid, Kevin."

"Call me, Cat," she says, shaking your hand. Then she steps back and rests her head on one of Nick's broad shoulders. "We were asleep when you called. Must have dozed off." She is wearing a pair of short shorts, a small top with thin straps, and sneakers. *Hmm, sporty.* Maybe she and Nick **work out** together at the gym.

"Sorry about that," you say, dragging your giant suitcase and duffel bag up behind you.

"Let me get that for you," Nick offers.

"How long do you plan to stay?" Cat asks, **trailing behind** Nick as he grunts up the stairs with your things. You watch as she gracefully walks up the stairs. Cat is incredibly beautiful—too beautiful.

*Something is **wrong with this picture**. How did Nick get a girl like her? She's **out of his league**.*

"I don't know," you answer. "A few weeks until school starts back home, I think." Cat **flashes** you a polite smile that makes your **stomach do flips**. "And how did you two meet?" you ask as you enter Nick's apartment.

"Facebook!" they say together.

"Through a friend, one of the waiters I work with," Cat adds. "I was browsing through his Friends list and saw this guy with pretty brown eyes and big muscles. So I requested him, and he added me. **The rest is history.**"

If you think that Cat means that the rest of the story of how they met is long and boring, go to **page 15**.

If you think that Cat means that it should be obvious what happened next, go to **page 16**.

Cat means that the rest of the story of how they met is long and boring—nothing special. *Or . . . does she not want to tell me the whole story?*

"Well, you might not think it's all that interesting, but I'd still like to hear it," you **prod her** politely. "Besides, I'm curious to know how my beast of a friend **ended up** with such a beauty." You wink teasingly at Nick.

Cat shrugs her shoulders. "There's not much else to say that you don't already know. It all happened so fast. We started sending each other messages. Then he started coming into the restaurant where I work. He was just so funny and charming that I couldn't resist."

"**Guilty as charged**—I am a charmer!" boasts your cousin. "I **swept her off her feet**."

"Then what happened?"

"Well, isn't it obvious?" Cat **narrows her eyes** at you briefly. She looks as if she is annoyed at your questions. Then she forces a laugh and kisses Nick on the forehead. Nick **beams with pride**.

You still have your suspicions, but Cat is probably telling you the truth. Nick has always been good at **putting on a show** for the ladies. That might simply be the rest of the story **after all**.

Go to **page 16**.

Cat means that it should be obvious what happened next. "Yeah, it's easy to see," you say. "You **fell in love** with him."

"Nah, I think she just likes me for my muscles," Nick says. Cat smiles and playfully squeezes his giant bicep.

Suddenly, your detective instincts **kick into overdrive**. How can they be **in love** if they just met? On Facebook of all places? There must be something more to this relationship. You examine Cat's sweet expression for signs that she is faking her feelings for your cousin, but you just can't tell.

Not yet anyway.

"Nick tells me you're also an actress," you say, trying to **mask your suspicion** and keep her talking.

"Trying to be," Cat corrects you. "I've only been in a few plays and independent films so far."

"She's very talented," Nick says. "Here, **sit down**. I'm sure you're tired after your long trip."

The couch already has a blanket and a pillow on it for you. *Since when is Nick so thoughtful?* **Taken aback** by Nick's unusual hospitality, you watch him carefully. Like Cat, he also seems happy. Could your cousin also be **putting on an act**?

"Are you hungry?" Nick asks you as he walks into the open kitchen.

You look around. The apartment is a cozy one-bedroom. There is a bar and some stools separating the kitchen from the living room where you are sitting. "A little," you lie.

"Well, I'll **heat up** some leftover lasagna that Cat brought over from the restaurant," Nick suggests. You watch your cousin as he briskly moves around in his kitchen with a big smile on his face. He seems happy you are here.

"That's a nice watch," Cat remarks. You are surprised when she sits right beside you on the couch. Your **heart beats** fast when you feel Cat's leg accidentally **brush against** yours. Before you can respond, she reaches for your hand. "What year is it from?"

You look down at your watch and consider the old timepiece made of quartz and glass. Although you aren't sure when it was made, you know it is valuable. Your mother sent it to you as a gift when you turned eighteen. You have worn the watch every day since, although the **time is off** by a few minutes. You are supposed to wind it **by hand** from **time to time**, but you often forget. In a way, you think that your neglect is a **silent protest** against your mother because she was always reminding you to **wind it up**.

"No one's asked me that before. I have no idea," you say honestly.

"Let me **take a look**. I **have a thing** for fashion and designer labels." She leans over your lap to examine your watch more closely. "That's strange. I don't see a brand name anywhere."

"Huh," you answer, shifting away from her on the couch. For some reason, for all her friendliness, this woman makes you feel uncomfortable. "I think it's an antique, maybe handmade."

"Wow—vintage!" she exclaims. "This one is vintage too." She shows you a large, blue gemstone ring on her right hand. "I just got this one at a **flea market**. It might be real sapphire. I'm an avid collector of vintage jewelry."

As her long hair falls on your arms, you **catch a whiff** of her perfume. You **jerk back** and **tense up**. You glance at Nick, but he is happily preparing your plate in the kitchen. He doesn't notice anything.

"Come closer," she says, squeezing next to you, "so I can see the detail on that watch. The leather wristband is in excellent condition."

Something vibrates in your pants—your phone. You jump, a little relieved for the distraction.

Cat laughs at you. "Are you okay?"

"Yeah, I just forgot something."

You **look down** and see that the number on the screen is **blocked**. Who would be calling this phone? The taxi driver? Someone who knows the taxi driver? Or could it be someone related to your mother's disappearance? Some **sixth sense** warns you to be careful.

"Please excuse me . . . " You don't finish explaining and run to the bathroom where you can answer the call **in private**. You close the door behind you.

"Hello?" you speak into the phone.

No answer.

"Hello?" you say again.

Worried it might be a **bad connection**, you try to move to the other corner of the bathroom, but all you can hear is **static** still. You try to get a **higher perch** by standing on top of the toilet seat. As you raise yourself up, your foot slips. You **knock over** a bottle of cologne. Shards of glass scatter on the floor.

"You okay? What's happening in there?" Cat asks outside the door.

"I'm fine." You stare at the floor. "I broke a glass bottle. It was empty though. Nothing spilled."

You put your ear against the phone. The **line is dead** now. With the number blocked, there is no way for you to return the call. Your **mind starts spinning** with a thousand ideas, some as far-fetched as any in your detective novels. A terrible thought occurs to you: *What if it was my mother on the phone?* You stare down at the phone. *No, it's impossible. This phone belonged to the taxi driver . . .*

You must be **jumping to conclusions**. Still shaking, you put the phone back in your pocket.

When you open the door, Cat strides in holding a broom and a dustpan. "Let me **clean it up** for you," Cat offers, wearing a sweet smile. Right in front of you, she bends down and begins **sweeping up** the broken glass.

By being eager to please or **borderline** flirtatious, she is trying to get your attention. Why is she sending you **mixed signals**?

If you think that Cat is definitely flirting with you, go to **page 19**.

If you think that Cat might be flirting with you, but you're not sure, go to **page 23**.

Cat is definitely flirting with you. In fact, she is trying to get your attention quite boldly. But why? You decide you need to **play her game** to see what she is really **up to**.

"Wait, Cat, let me get that," you say, kneeling beside her. You set down your smartphone on the bathroom floor. You notice her looking too long at the screen. "I can't bear to watch a pretty lady on the ground cleaning up *my* mess."

She stops sweeping and playfully holds the dustpan and broom behind her back so you can't reach it. "You're a guest. I wouldn't think of it."

You smile and lean toward her, trying to snatch the dustpan and broom. "Let me be a gentleman."

"Never!"

You are both laughing when the bathroom door swings opens.

"What's **going on** here?" Nick is frowning at the both of you.

You awkwardly hit your heads together when you both try to **stand up** at the same time.

"Am I interrupting something?" Nick scowls. His expression reminds you **of the days** when you were teenagers, competing for **the girl next door**. He never liked it when he wasn't the **center of attention**.

"No, we're just . . . " you start to say.

"I was just helping Kevin with . . . " Cat tries to finish.

You aren't sure why you are both **tongue-tied** when your interaction in the bathroom was quite innocent. You try to explain what happened. You pick up the smartphone and hold it up to show Nick the blocked phone number on the screen.

"I **knocked over** a glass bottle trying to get a signal," you manage to say.

"And so I brought him a dustpan and broom and offered to **clean it up**," Cat adds.

"How sweet of you, Cat," Nick says sarcastically. He looks at you. "Well, who was it?"

"Who was who?" You feel your face **turn red**, something you always do uncontrollably when you are hiding something.

Nick **narrows his eyes**. "On the phone."

"Oh, right. I don't know. I answered, but no one was there." You are so **rattled by** Nick's reaction that you drop your phone again.

He crosses his arms and nods slowly. It looks as if he just realized something. "Well, I guess I should just let you two finish whatever it was you started."

When he walks out, Cat looks at you apologetically. She grabs your phone and gives it back to you. "Don't worry about Nick. He'll be okay. He has a few **hang ups** sometimes and then gets annoyed and stays in a bad mood."

If you think that Cat is saying that Nick is often worried about her talking to other men, go to **page 21**.

If you think that Cat is talking about rude callers, go to **page 22**.

Cat is saying that Nick is often worried about her talking to other men. You aren't surprised considering Nick's **jealous streak**. You nod with understanding and slowly help her to her feet. As you pull her up, you feel her squeeze your hand. Nervously, you pull your hand away.

"You know what? I'm pretty tired," you say. "I think I'm going to eat some of that lasagna and then go to bed."

"Oh, I'm sure it's cold by now. Let me go **heat it up** for you in the microwave," Cat offers.

While the lasagna is being heated for the second time, you **sit down** next to Nick who is watching TV on the couch.

"I'm sorry about what happened in the bathroom," you say to him quietly. "I wasn't expecting that phone call."

Go to **page 24**.

Cat is talking about rude callers who **hang up** when Nick answers the phone. Has your cousin also been getting strange **prank** phone calls?

"Really? He gets **hang ups**?" you ask. "Who do you think keeps calling and **hanging up**?"

"Not on the phone, silly," Cat says. "He's just jealous. He doesn't like it when I talk to other men. I guess not even his best friend."

You realize how bad the situation must have looked to Nick. He thought you were **hitting on** his girlfriend.

"I'll talk to him," you reassure Cat, **helping her to her feet**. "He has no reason to be **hung up** on us."

"Definitely not."

When you both walk out of the bathroom, Cat busies herself in the kitchen while you **sit down** next to Nick on the couch.

"I hope you know there's nothing to worry about," you tell him as he keeps his eyes **fixed on** the TV. "Cat was just trying to be helpful. That's all."

Go to **page 24**.

Cat might be flirting with you. However, she did say she is an actress-in-training. Aren't actresses supposed to be dramatic? Maybe she isn't flirting and is just being herself. Besides, Cat seems to be **head over heels in love** with Nick anyway.

"What happened in there?" Nick yells from the kitchen.

"Nothing, sweetie," Cat shouts back, answering for you. "Kevin just had a little accident. I **took care of it**." She smiles at you with her perfect teeth. "Are you sure you're okay, Kevin?"

"I'm just tired from the flight," you say, walking back to the couch and **falling down** on it. "I'm not even hungry anymore. I just need to go to bed, guys."

As Nick walks toward you with a plate of lasagna, Cat stops him, rubbing his back.

"What's wrong with him?" Nick asks her.

"Nothing, sweetie. **Go easy on him**. He's just had a long trip. Let Kevin get some rest."

Nick lets Cat lead him toward the bedroom. He stops to put the lasagna back in the refrigerator. "If you **change your mind** and get hungry, you know where the **grub** is," he says to you. "**Help yourself** and **feel at home**."

You **nod back**. "Thanks for everything, Nick."

Go to **page 25**.

You **can't help but** wonder when you and your cousin will get a chance to talk about your mother. You open your mouth to say something, but Nick **talks over** you.

"No problem," he says with a yawn, turning his back to you and **heading** into the bedroom with Cat. "Oh, before I forget . . . " He reaches into his pocket and tosses you keys. "You might not see me much these days since my work schedule is crazy this time of year, but you can **come and go** as you please. Just **make yourself at home**, Kiddo."

He doesn't **catch his mistake** in calling you 'Kiddo,' but you are pretty sure that Cat noticed.

Go to **page 25**.

In the morning, the first thing you do when you **wake up** is to check your phone. You are anxious to see if there are any new missed calls. You examine all the **icons** on the screen and notice an app for Facebook. When you **sign in**, you are surprised to see a message from an anonymous account.

> Hello. I work with your mother. Meet me at Miss Larsen's Laundromat @ 12pm today to take care of some **dirty laundry**.

This is your **first lead**, so you decide to **go for it**.

At noon, you stand outside Miss Larsen's Laundromat, not sure who you are looking for. There are several people inside doing their laundry, but no one is **paying attention** to you. Then you notice one woman who is busy cleaning the floor. Using her mop, she **makes her way** toward you. She is a tall woman in her early forties with broad shoulders and short black hair. She **looks** physically fit—like an Olympic swimmer.

"Betty Rogers," the woman says, holding out her hand to you. "I worked with your mother at Cleaning House, Inc., but we were also friends. Thank you for meeting me."

"I'm David," you say, shaking her hand.

"Nice to meet you. **Walk this way**." She points in the direction of a row of washing machines and dryers at the far end of the room. "We can't **draw attention** to ourselves, so we'll do some laundry."

You follow her over to a basket of laundry and help her throw bed sheets and pillowcases into one of the washing machines.

"So," she says, pouring some detergent into the machine. "Do you have any idea about what has happened to your mother?"

You tell her what you know. "My cousin told me she disappeared. I think maybe she reported a client to the authorities and now that person is **after her**. I was hoping you could **fill me in** on the rest. What do you know?"

Betty nods thoughtfully. "Normally, your mother is very good at what she does and can **get out of** these situations. But this time, it looks like she got herself into serious trouble." She looks at you. "David, your mother has **put a lot of confidence in you**. The way she talked about you . . . I think you might know something or have something that will help us find her."

You remember how Nick said your mother asked for you specifically. But you still **have no clue** why that could be. "Betty, **there must be some mistake**. My mother and I have been separated for fifteen years now. I don't have anything or know anything about her life here that would help. I'm **in the dark** more than you."

Betty peers at you with doubt. She looks both worried and impatient. You feel helpless. Even though everyone seems to think you can do something useful, you don't think you have anything to offer.

"I know this is a lot to **take in**," she says. "Let me explain." She pushes the start button on the washing machine next to you. The machine makes loud clinking and clanking sounds as it **starts up**. It is so loud that you can hardly **hear yourself think**. Betty moves closer to you until she is whispering near your ear. "Your mother never told you who we are, did she?"

You shake your head.

"Cleaning House, Inc. isn't just an ordinary cleaning agency, David," Betty says. "Our 'housekeepers' do more than just clean rooms. We **clean house**."

If you think that Betty means that Cleaning House, Inc. goes to people's homes and cleans them, go to **page 27**.

If you think that Betty means that Cleaning House, Inc. solves cases, go to **page 28**.

Betty means that Cleaning House, Inc. goes to people's homes and cleans them. *Well, that's obvious.*

She waits for a **sign** of understanding on your face, but you just stare at her blankly. Her eyes **dart around** the room, and then she turns to you. "We're a special kind of detective agency," she says slowly. "Your mother is an agent of ours. She **cleans house**. Do you understand? She **goes undercover** to solve cases."

"What?" you laugh nervously. You think she must be joking, but Betty's expression doesn't change.

Oh.

Go to **page 28.**

Betty means that Cleaning House, Inc. solves cases; it isn't an ordinary cleaning agency that goes around and cleans people's homes and offices. You can hardly believe it.

"She isn't a cleaning lady?"

Betty smiles knowingly. "Ana was once. When she first moved to the U.S., she was the housekeeper of a wealthy family down in Houston, Texas—the Fosters. Frederick Foster III was a successful businessman and computer engineer. He was married with a wife and daughter. Did Ana ever talk about them?"

You do remember your mother telling you about a family she worked for in Houston. She didn't talk very much about the parents, but she often talked fondly about a little girl who was **around your age** at the time. It made you jealous, so you often didn't **pay much attention** to what she said about the girl. In fact, you don't even remember her real name; your mother always used a nickname.

"She talked about a little girl before, I think. She loved her like a daughter from what I can recall."

Betty nods. "Yes, well, Ana was very close to the family . . . until she discovered Frederick Foster's secret. Foster was a wealthy man who owned many businesses. Unfortunately, one of those businesses happened to be a shipping business for a **drug ring**. When your mother found evidence of his involvement with the drug trade while cleaning his home office, she told the police and the FBI. It was all over the news." For a moment, she looks at you, puzzled. "I'm surprised you didn't know about it."

Speechless, you just shake your head. Your mother never mentioned it, and you hardly **pay any attention** to **current events** or the news. You have always **lived your life through** books and movies.

"Foster went to prison. Soon after, your mother was placed in a **witness protection program**. After that, Foster's wife divorced him and **ran away** with their young daughter and everything they had, including a fortune that's now **in his daughter's name**. According to our **sources** in prison, he loved his daughter **more than anything in the world**. He wrote her letters every day. Sadly, the letters would be sent back to him unopened." Betty stops and lowers her voice even more. "He almost killed himself because of it."

"If my mother was just a housekeeper for the Fosters, how did she end up working for you?"

"When I heard about Foster's case on the news, I brought it **to the attention** of our chief. We recruited her and brought her here to Washington, D.C. She's a very talented investigator—observant, **quick on her feet**. Cleaning House was lucky to have her."

'Was' lucky to have her instead of 'is'? Betty is talking as if your mother will never work for Cleaning House again, like she is **gone for good**.

"I know she took her job very seriously. I just didn't know it was *this* kind of job."

Betty's face darkens. "No one **saw it coming**. We think Foster **tracked down** your mother as soon as he got out of prison for good behavior. Our agents were following him down in Texas—until one day he simply **fell off the grid** and disappeared. Then our sources saw him here in D.C. He may be working under an alias, a fake name."

"So you suspect that this Frederick Foster is responsible for kidnapping my mother out of revenge?"

She holds up her hands. "We don't want to **jump to any conclusions**. We're not sure what his involvement might be. But Frederick Foster is our best **lead** right now. He's a very intelligent man with many connections. He also has **unfinished business** with your mother. I think he blames her for everything that's happened to him. He's got the best **motive** for kidnapping her."

Everything Betty has revealed overwhelms you. You **wring your hands** in frustration. "How does my mother think I can help her?"

"To be honest, we're not sure. But your mother talked about you all the time. She told us about the mystery games you'd play, and how quick you were at following her clues or solving the riddles she'd give you."

You nod. It is true. Before you could even read, your mother taught you how to decode pictures and symbols and even how to **make up** your own—all using the hieroglyphs from a copy of a **Mayan codex** she owned. It was one of her most treasured possessions. A kind of illustrated dictionary, the codex was filled with glyphs, or a set of symbols. From then on, your mother would teach you **little by little** what some of those symbols meant and use them as clues.

From your experience with the codex, you learned that anything used to communicate—simple words and expressions—could have multiple meanings. You were five or six years old when you first realized this. Your mother had just finished baking your favorite cookies. Although you wanted to eat them right out of the oven, your mother told you they needed to **cool down** first. You went outside to play. When you came back, the cookies were all gone. You burst into tears. You demanded to know who ate the cookies.

"I can't tell you exactly who it was, but I'll give you a hint," she said. "If you get it right, this person will bake you two batches of your favorite cookies."

Your eyes got wide, and you stopped crying immediately.

"Are you ready? This person can sometimes be **short on patience**. Can you guess who it is?"

You thought hard about this piece of information. Everyone in your family was known to be short on patience, including you. The fact that you wanted the cookies right out of the oven showed that you were **short on patience**. You thought about everyone living in the house. The only other person at home at this time was your grandfather. But he wasn't that impatient. As a dentist, he had to show a lot of patience.

Then it **hit you**. Your grandfather, who was the only dentist in town, used to joke that he never had enough patients because no one liked to visit the dentist. Your mother meant "short on patients," not "short on patience." Even at a young age, you realized that sometimes you need to **read between the lines** to understand what someone is really saying.

"You see, David," Betty continues, interrupting your memories, "you and your mother have a special connection. If she tries to reach out to us somehow, she'll probably use a coded message that won't be obvious to anyone else but you. That's why we need your help. You may be the only person who'd be able to understand."

"I don't know," you say doubtfully.

"David," Betty urges. "We need to find out if Frederick Foster is responsible for Ana's disappearance. It's all **up to you** now."

It's all up to me . . . You recall how Nick said the same thing to you over the phone. Something doesn't feel right, but you can't **put your finger on it**.

The washing machine screeches louder now, forcing both of you to cover your ears. Then Betty looks at you, frowning. "Time to **take matters into your own hands**."

If you think that Betty is asking you to consider your lack of experience and get training first, go to **page 33**.

If you think that Betty is trying to get you to agree to join the mission, go to **page 37**.

[CHAPTER TWO]

~ Second Thoughts

BETTY IS ASKING you to consider your lack of experience and get training first. To you, **taking matters into your own hands** means being prepared.

"Betty, I really want to help you find my mother," you begin slowly. "That's why I came here **in the first place**. But I'm also comfortable admitting that I need to **learn the basics** first. Without training, I might **blow this whole mission**."

Betty nods sympathetically. "Yes, I think you're right, David," she says. "You should have some training before we send you on a mission. The problem is we don't have a lot of time before we need to **drop you in the deep end**. If we take too long, it might give Foster some time to escape before we can question him."

She takes your hands and squeezes them. Her hands feel warm and comforting.

"Go home tonight and **sleep on it**. **Make sure** you think you can handle this **on your own**. After all, you can't involve anyone else in this—not even your cousin. I know he's family, but if he finds out, he could put you, your mission, and your mother in danger. In the morning, you'll receive a message from another anonymous

Facebook account with a time and location for where to meet me . . . if you're ready."

Maybe Betty is right. Since you arrived last night, this has all been **a whirlwind**, and you may just need some more time to think this through.

You are about to thank her when the washing machine next to you starts rattling loudly. You look at each other and then at the machine. Betty opens the top of the washer and starts fishing through the soapy water for something.

Immediately, you **roll up your sleeves**. You may have disappointed Betty about the mission, but hopefully you can **come to the rescue** for a mechanical issue. You do **have a knack** for fixing things.

"Please let me help," you offer.

"I think there's something jammed deep under the **agitator**. I might **need a hand with this**. **Do you mind**?"

"Not at all."

Betty steps **out of the way**. When you start to **reach in** with both your hands, Betty stops you. "Don't you want to take that off first?" she asks, pointing to your left wrist.

You realize that she is talking about your watch. "Good idea," you say, relieved. "It was a gift from my mother. It's old, too. Definitely not waterproof. I need to be more careful with it."

You take your watch off and set it carefully on top of the washing machine beside you. Your wrist now bare, you reach into the clogged machine, feeling around the base of the agitator. Eventually, your fingers find a tiny, metal object. You twist and turn it until you feel it **break free**. "Got it!" you shout triumphantly, holding the object tightly in your fist.

When you open your hand, you discover a well-worn, silver ring with some sort of symbol carved into a green stone. The color of the stone looks familiar. It is similar to the common jade stone that you often see in Mayan jewelry.

"Thank you so much," Betty says, snatching the ring out of your hand. She puts it in her pocket before you can **get a closer look**. "I've been looking for that everywhere. I thought I'd lost it. How careless of me!"

You smile, happy to be **of service** to this woman who seems so **put together**. "Sure. Glad I could help."

As you are about to leave, you stop at the entrance. You notice your **bare wrist**. "Wait—my watch."

You see Betty look at you blankly and cross her arms. "I almost forgot it," you say, looking around at the washing machines. "I placed my watch here after I **took it off**."

Not knowing why, you feel your face **turn red**. Again, you feel foolish in front Betty. As you try to avoid her **hard gaze**, your **eyes wander** to her hands. Betty is patting down her pockets nervously. Your **gaze lingers**, and this seems to startle her.

"Oh, here it is—**safe and sound**," she blurts out. "I thought you might forget it. I must have **slipped** it into my pocket **for safekeeping** without thinking." With one smooth move, she returns your watch to your wrist.

"Thanks," you say.

As you turn to leave, you can feel Betty's watchful eyes behind you, watching **every move you make**. Her **vigilance** is oddly comforting, if a bit unsettling. Then your **mind wanders** back to the ring that got stuck in the washing machine. Cat also wore a ring like that, though that one had a blue stone. Betty's ring is **made out of** jade, which isn't unusual, but it reminds you of a ring your mother also wore. You were going to mention that to Betty, but then you stopped when you realized that she didn't put the ring back on. Why did she just put it in her pocket?

You think about your watch. *Why did Betty put my watch in her pocket?* She claimed she forgot to give it back to you. But Betty doesn't **strike you** as the type of person to forget things so easily. You don't really **buy her story**.

You sigh. Your mind is filled with questions and conflicting thoughts. Maybe it is time to **take a walk** to **clear your head** before going back to Nick's apartment. You are relieved that your detective skills are finally coming back to you, and yet you feel bad for letting your suspicions **get the best of you**. After just meeting Betty, you are already **pointing fingers**.

Go to **page 43**.

Betty is trying to get you to agree to join the mission. You feel the pressure. Your mother is **counting on you,** and it is time you **showed some initiative**.

A few days ago, you were just a kid in college. The most exciting thing that happened to you before you left for the States was getting to meet one of your crime novel authors at a **book signing**. Now, a highly trained undercover agent wants you to join her investigation to find your mother.

"I'm **in,**" you answer finally. *If people from home could see me now . . .*

Betty squeezes your hand before you can protest again. "I need to show you something, but I don't want you to be alarmed or to **jump to any conclusions**." She pulls out a clear plastic bag. Inside it is a silver ring with a jade stone. "Was this your mother's?"

The ring looks familiar. Betty places the bag in your hand, and you stare at it for a long time. The ring is heavy and well-worn. Through the plastic you can see that the stone has a Mayan carving. Your mother loved Mayan art. She constantly talked about Mayan symbols and patterns and what they meant.

"It might be hers. I don't know."

"We found it on the floor in her living room. We are examining it for fingerprints at our headquarters. It looks like there was a struggle, or maybe she left it **on purpose**—as a clue."

A hard **lump forms in your throat** as you **fight back tears**. You turn away, embarrassed.

Betty grabs your wrist. "What's this?" Without waiting for you to answer, she takes the watch off your wrist in one easy move.

"What are you doing?" *First Cat, now Betty—everyone is obsessed with my watch.*

From her purse, she takes out a tiny toolkit. "Did your mother give you this watch?"

You become suspicious. "It was a birthday present."

"Remarkable. It's a watch built for undercover work," Betty says.

Skillfully, she pries open the glass cover with a metal pin and examines the inside of the watch as if she is looking for something. She takes out a small jeweler's loupe, a tiny magnifying glass, and peers inside the watch. You **lean in** closer to **take a look**.

"See?" With the loupe, she shows you a gap between the gears underneath the glass plate. "You can hide things here. Fascinating. I think that's why Ana gave it to you. She probably knew you might need it one day."

"Why would I need a watch like this?"

"For something like this maybe?" With her other hand, Betty takes out a small microchip. "It's just a **tracking device**," she explains, anticipating your question. "We can use it to follow your every move. **No matter** where you are, one of our agents will be **close by**. See this tiny button on the side of the watch? Push this button if you're ever in immediate danger. It will activate the tracker."

"Danger?" you say. You imagine yourself being **trigger-happy**, pressing the button at every opportunity.

Betty seems to **read your thoughts**. "But make sure you use it with caution. It needs to be a *real* emergency because our detectives **have a lot on their plates** with other cases. Once you push the button, someone will be there in minutes."

An emergency button? Agents tracking your every move? It all sounds like something out of your crime novels. "I—I don't know. I'm **out of my league** here," you stammer.

"Now isn't the time to be scared," Betty says, forcefully putting the watch back on you—though on your other wrist. She doesn't seem to realize her mistake. "We'll have undercover teams—people dressed like ordinary folks—protecting you at all times. Do you still have the phone the taxi driver gave you?"

Your eyes open wide. "What? The taxi driver was part of Cleaning House, Inc.?" No wonder the man was so quick to offer you his phone.

"Like I said, we **have you covered**. Here's how this will work: When we get a new **lead** about Foster or your mother, we'll send you a clue through Facebook about where to go next. No phone calls."

You think about the strange blocked phone call at Nick's apartment. You want to ask her about it, but she continues with her instructions. Betty isn't the kind of person you interrupt so easily.

"We customized your Facebook account." She raises her hand when she sees the look of shock on your face. "Don't ask how. Our tech people are skilled. The security settings we installed will make sure no one can **hack** into your messages and read things without your knowledge."

You look at her, impressed. "This network of yours . . . How will I know who is there to help me?"

She smiles. "Cleaning House, Inc. uses a special signal: three short sweeps, three long sweeps."

Betty grabs a broom from behind one of the washing machines and demonstrates the exact sweeping motion. It is the same action you saw her do with the mop when you came in. Then you remember how Cat used a broom to **sweep up** the glass from the bathroom floor. *Was she giving me the signal?* You try to remember whether you saw a pattern in her sweeping, but it is all a blur.

Betty senses that you are still unsure. "I know this is a lot to think about right now. You'll get your first mission tonight. Your mother wanted this, David. If she trusts you, then we trust you."

Next to you, the washing machine starts to shift and rock, switching cycles from wash to rinse.

Betty leans in closer. "You can really **hold up** this investigation."

If you think that Betty is saying that you will hinder the investigation, go to **page 40**.

If you think that Betty is saying that you can support the investigation, go to **page 42**.

Betty is saying that you will hinder the investigation—especially with your lack of confidence.

"But I'm ready," you insist. Your voice rises above the sound of the washing machines. You want to prove to Betty that you can do this, that you can be an undercover detective and **clean house**, just like your mother.

Betty frowns and signals for you to lower your voice. "Okay, okay. But you need to keep a **low profile**, David. Ever wonder why we decided on Cleaning House as our **cover**? Cleaners and housekeepers tend to **blend in**. We don't attract attention. This is dangerous work. **Make the wrong move,** and you can definitely make things difficult for us and **hold up** the investigation."

Without turning her head, Betty's eyes look to the left at a woman next to you doing her laundry. Slowly, you follow Betty's gaze. You aren't sure why Betty is worried about this stranger. The other woman doesn't seem to notice you as she pauses to check her phone. She continues putting her laundry in the washing machine.

"On the count of three," Betty whispers to you, her mouth barely moving. I want you to block the door to the entrance."

Your eyes grow big.

"One, two—"

Before Betty gets to the count of three, the woman drops her laundry and runs for the door. Luckily, you are closer and reach the door a second faster than she does. With all your strength, you **hold the door shut**. The woman lunges at you, but Betty tackles her from behind. She wrestles the woman to the ground and twists her arms behind her back. To secure her, Betty **digs her knees** into the woman's side.

"**Do me a favor**," Betty says, looking up at you. "Call the agency and ask for **backup**. Hurry! The number is preset on your phone. Cleaning House, Inc."

Although in shock, you do what she says. "They're **on their way**," you tell her, after you **make contact**.

A crowd of people starts to gather around Betty and the woman, whispering and pointing. "Nothing to see here, folks," Betty tells the people. "Official police business. Move along, move along." The onlookers look disappointed but slowly step away.

"Who are you? Who sent you? Tell me," Betty growls into the woman's ear.

The woman shakes her head and says nothing. Betty twists her arms harder, making the woman scream, but the woman still refuses to say anything.

Desperate, Betty searches the woman's pockets. With only one hand holding down the woman's arms, Betty **loses her grip**. The woman thrashes, knocking Betty off balance. Betty goes for her gun, but it is too late. The woman is already **dashing out** of the Laundromat.

"Should we go after her?" you ask, still shocked at what you just witnessed. Everything happened so fast, in the **blink of an eye**.

"It's alright. We have this." Betty waves the woman's wallet. From inside its folds, she pulls out a piece of paper and shows it to you.

FBI Headquarters

The Federal Bureau of Investigation—the Feds?

Your heart beats faster as you realize how dangerous this mission really is. It isn't just playacting and eavesdropping, or pretending to be a cleaner. It is also defending yourself against attacks and chasing down suspects.

Do you really have what it takes to **clean house**?

Go to **page 43**.

Betty is saying that you can support and help the investigation. "I'll do my best to **hold up** this investigation," you answer. "All I want to do is help."

"**That's the spirit**," Betty praises you. "We're going to make a great team. And more importantly, we're going to get Frederick Foster and **put him away for good**."

You can see Betty's face **harden with determination**.

"And find my mother," you add. "Right?"

Betty's face twitches. You make a **mental note**. She gives you a quick smile, but her eyes **stay serious**.

"Of course. And find Ana, too."

As soon as you leave the Laundromat, your confidence fades. For a few hours, you wander around the city, thinking of all the things that could go wrong: *What if I can't follow Betty's orders? What if I push the emergency button on my watch, but Betty's team can't find me in time? What if it's already too late?*

You shudder at the terrible thoughts.

Go to **page 43**.

After the meeting with Betty, you decide to **take a walk**. You look at a map and decide to **check out** the sidewalk shops in Georgetown and **kill time** before you go back to Nick's apartment. You are about to **take a peek** inside the Nike Factory store, when you hear a familiar voice.

"Kevin, Kevin!"

You freeze and look over your shoulder. From the **corner of your eye**, you see a figure standing on the corner of Wisconsin Avenue. The person is waving at you even though her arms are loaded with shopping bags.

It is Cat.

"Kevin!" she calls out to you again.

Even in her T-shirt, frayed skinny jeans, and white sneakers, she still looks as **stunning** as ever. She flashes you a big smile when you finally wave back.

"Hey! I thought that was you," she says when she reaches you. "I've been trying to **catch your eye**. Are you trying to avoid me?"

You try to reply with a good excuse. "**Jetlag** must be **messing with** my mind. I'm still pretty **beat** from the trip."

"Aww," she says, nodding. She **sets down** her bags and squeezes your shoulder.

"What are you doing in this part of the city? Don't you work **across town** at the restaurant?" It seems unusual that Cat has **shown up** right where you **happen to be**.

"I know. I left work a little early today, so I decided to go shopping." She jiggles her shopping bags and groans. "As you can see, I got **carried away**. Can you help?"

If you think that Cat got distracted and lost her way while shopping, go to **page 44**.

If you think that Cat got excited about shopping and bought too many things, go to **page 45**.

Cat got distracted and lost her way while shopping it seems.

"No, I don't mind at all," you answer politely, trying to be a gentleman.

She gives you three bags to carry in each hand and keeps one for herself. Then, to your surprise, she leads the way to bus stop.

"Are you sure you know where you're going now?" you ask her. "Maybe we should stop and look at a map first."

She **looks at you sideways**. "Of course I know where I'm going. I live here. You're the one from **out of town**."

Now you are confused. Did you say something rude? She shakes her head and starts walking faster, so you have to hurry to follow her.

"Hey, I'm sorry I got a little impatient with you," she says once you both reach the bus stop. "I was just embarrassed. I don't usually get **carried away** and buy so many things. But I thought I deserved a little **splurge** since I got the new waitressing job."

Go to **page 45**.

Cat got excited about shopping and bought too many things. You wonder how she can get **carried away** and afford such a **shopping spree** on a waitress's salary. Nick has always been a **cheapskate**, and yet he must have given her some money to go shopping. It is yet another sign that he is **madly in love** with Cat.

"Kevin, do you mind helping me carry these bags home . . . since we're going in the same direction?"

"Sure." You take three bags for each of your hands, while she keeps one to carry herself.

"Nick is going to **kill me** when he gets home."

As you wait with Cat at the bus stop, you wonder when you and your cousin will finally get the chance to talk. Although Betty warned you not to get him involved and to be careful about how much you tell him, you do want to share your thoughts about your mother with someone. It is the one thing you and Nick **have in common**. But if Cat is always in the apartment, there is no way for you to **bring up** your mother at all.

Next to you Cat **clears her throat**. "Here comes our bus."

Sitting together on the bus, you try to pretend to listen to her stories about the latest fashion and celebrity news. As Cat continues talking, you glance at her shopping bags. You notice something odd when you peek inside. Instead of new designer clothes and accessories with tags and receipts, you see piles of folded laundry, mostly bed sheets and pillowcases. Immediately, you think about your meeting with Betty at Miss Larsen's Laundromat. Wasn't Betty washing loads of white sheets?

You think about what you know about Cat. Right now, other than the **funny feeling** you have when you are with her, you don't have any real evidence that she is anything other than Nick's girlfriend. Maybe it was just a **coincidence** that you ran into her at the shopping center. But D.C. is a big city. Why was she so far away from the restaurant where she works? If she wanted to go shopping after work, wouldn't she go somewhere nearby?

"Are you still listening?" Cat asks, interrupting your thoughts.

"Um, yeah. **Carry on**."

Cat laughs nervously and moves uncomfortably in her seat. "I'm sorry if I'm boring you with all of my **girl talk**. I'm sure you don't think skinny jeans and celebrity babies are very interesting."

"No, it's alright," you say, feeling your face **turn red**.

She smiles, leaning in closer to you. "Let's talk more about how you know Nick. How did you two first meet?"

"Oh, I don't know," you say, trying to think of a story that sounds believable. "It was so long ago. We were in grade school together in the same class. We liked the same girl. We always fought about girls."

"That's odd," Cat replies, looking out the bus window. "Nick told me you two met in high school, playing soccer."

Cat talked to Nick about you. And, of course, Nick wasn't smart enough to **change the subject** or coordinate a story with you.

You cough into your hand, trying to **stall for time** as you think of an explanation. "Well, we became close friends in high school when we played on the soccer team together. But we first met in grade school. He probably doesn't remember. You know Nick!"

"What was the name of your soccer team again?"

Now you are almost sure Cat is testing you. Luckily, you really did play on the same team, even if you didn't play during the same year as your cousin. "The Lions," you answer. She seems satisfied and is quiet until you get to your stop.

When you finally get to the front door of Nick's apartment, you put down all of her bags so you can look for the key in your pockets. You feel Cat's eyes on you.

"You're a **lefty**," Cat says suddenly.

"Huh?"

"Left-handed." She points at your wrist. "Me, too."

Your **heart pounds** as you remember Betty putting back your watch on the wrong wrist. It must look **out of the ordinary**. Cat notices everything.

"Yesterday, I noticed your watch was on your left wrist, but today it's on your right, which is the wrist I wear my own watch on. Huh."

"Oh, no, I'm right-handed," you explain. "But it doesn't matter to me. I get, um, bored if I keep it on the same wrist all the time."

Cat stops smiling. "Are you **putting me on** right now?"

"What? No—"

"I'm just **playing with you!**" Cat exclaims, her gorgeous smile returning. "You're just like Nick—can't take a joke. Funny how similar you guys are. Like you're family—brothers or something."

You laugh nervously. Cat really doesn't miss *anything*. With all her questions, she could be **fishing for something**, trying to get more information. You will have to be extra careful around her.

Once inside Nick's apartment, you are disappointed to see that your cousin isn't home yet.

"Oh, I forgot to tell you," says Cat, sensing your unease. "Nick called me earlier. He's working **overtime**. He's **bummed** he won't be home early to **hang out** with you." She runs into the kitchen and opens the refrigerator. "So it looks like it'll just be us for dinner tonight. Is there anything you're **in the mood for**?"

"What?" you ask nervously. *Is she flirting with me again?*

"What do you want to eat?"

"Oh, nothing really."

"**Come on**, honey. Tell me what you want."

You shrug. "Oh, whatever." Luckily, Cat has already started to prepare something.

Suddenly, your phone starts to vibrate in your pocket. You are glad for the interruption—anything to distract you from Cat's constant questioning. **Holding your breath**, you click the message icon that has appeared.

> **You're on**. Go to the FBI Headquarters. Report to the housekeeping staff manager @ 7pm tomorrow night to start the **night shift**.

I'm on. The mission is finally happening—your first job as a bona fide undercover detective! You can't believe it. Naturally, of course, you have **butterflies in your stomach**.

If you are too nervous and need more time to think things through, go to **page 49**.

If you are excited about the mission, go to **page 53**.

You are too nervous and need more time to think things through. After a **stroll around** the neighborhood to **get rid of the butterflies in your stomach**, you return to Nick's apartment, calmer. While the walk did help to refresh you a bit and organize your thoughts, you still feel unsure, nervous.

Cat greets you in the living room. "Nick called again. He's **pulling another shift**," Cat announces, her eyes **fixed on** the TV as she **clicks through** the channels. "It's just us."

You frown to yourself. *Typical of Nick. Thinking more about* **making money** *than being there for me. Isn't he worried at all about finding my mother?*

"Everything okay?" Cat asks, interrupting your thoughts. "You're not looking so good."

"I just haven't seen much of Nick since I came here," you answer.

"**Cheer up.** You'll see him in the morning. **Midnight snack?**"

"Yeah, I can eat a little bit," you lie. Since you arrived in D.C., you haven't had much of an appetite.

"Well I can **fix that**," she answers, moving to the kitchen. "How about some leftover eggplant parmesan?"

"Sure," you say, collapsing onto the couch.

You are glad Cat is now far away enough that you can send Betty a message **in private**. You take out your smartphone and type a brief message.

> Not sure if I'm ready. I'm having **second thoughts**.

You are waiting for a response from Betty, when Cat yells to get your attention. The outburst nearly makes you drop your phone. Cat has a special way of startling you.

"Do you know what might **cheer** Nick **up**? Let's take a **selfie** together and post it on Facebook. We can add a caption that says, 'Look who's being replaced' or something like that."

"I don't think that would be a good idea."

"**Come on**, it'll be fun," she insists, already standing beside you. "Nick will **get a kick out of this** for sure."

"Hey . . . " you start to say as you try to **block yourself**, but you realize it is too late.

Cat clicks the camera on her phone several times. When you look over her shoulder to catch a glimpse of the photo, you see that it isn't a very good picture of you at all. Instead of looking like you are **in on the joke**, you look angry and confused. In fact, you look like you have been **caught in the act**. You don't think it is funny at all, but Cat is right—Nick might **get a kick** out of seeing such a horrible photo of you.

"Please don't post it," you beg. "I look awful."

"Where's your **sense of humor**? Let's take some more."

Although Cat is laughing, her demands seem like threats. She chases you around the living room, ignoring your protests and **shooting** picture after picture, even as you try to run and hide and cover your face. You are supposed to be undercover and now there are photos of you **floating around** the Internet. Not only that, you are sure to **get pounded** by Nick as soon as he comes home.

"**Come on!**" you yell.

Luckily, the smell of burning eggplant stops Cat **in her tracks**. "Shit!" She puts her phone in her pocket and rushes over to the oven, opening it and fanning the smoke. "It's ruined!"

"It's okay," you answer, relieved. "I'm not that hungry anymore."

Part of you wants to get as far away from Cat as possible, but at this point you are too tired to leave the apartment again. You grab a book and pretend to read until Nick gets home. Soon you fall asleep.

Go to **page 51**.

You awaken to the sound of the front door opening and Nick calling out. "Honey, I'm home!" You open your eyes to see Cat do a running leap into his arms. You groan and look at the clock on your smartphone. It is two o'clock in the morning.

"Sorry I'm so late," Nick says to Cat. "Some of the workers didn't show up, so I had to work **overtime**."

"No worries," Cat answers. "Kevin here entertained me, didn't you Kevin?"

"Is that so?" Nick says in your direction.

You smile weakly, not sure how to **take his words**.

"Yep," Cat answers for you. "Tell him what we did, Kevin."

"Um—didn't you see our **selfie** on Facebook?" you say to your cousin.

Nick pauses, the smile leaving his face. "Selfie?" He looks at Cat for help. It seems as if he doesn't know how he should react.

Cat shakes her head at him in disbelief. "**Come on**, darling," she says. There is an **edge to her voice**. "You're always checking Facebook, right?"

"So you didn't see it?" you say to Nick.

"Wait," Nick says, snapping his fingers. He and Cat **exchange strange looks.** Then he looks at you and lets out an exaggerated laugh. "Yeah, of course! I think **everyone and their mother** saw that picture."

Now you are suspicious. Knowing how jealous Nick can get, you know that his reaction is **off the mark**. If you were still teenagers, he would have had you on the ground already, and you would be begging for him to let you go. Just yesterday he was upset about Cat laughing with you in the bathroom. Strangely, Cat's mood has also changed. She gestures sternly for Nick to hurry into the bedroom with her.

"Uh, we'll have to **catch up** tomorrow before I go to work," Nick says, his mouth full of food as he follows Cat into the bedroom.

"Good night," you answer quietly, still feeling uncertain.

Behind the bedroom door, Cat and Nick continue to argue in hushed tones. You can't hear what they are saying, and you wonder if it has anything to do with you and the Facebook **selfie**. You try to forget about it and go to sleep.

The next morning, your phone beeps with a message from Betty.

Ready to **get your feet wet**? Meet the housekeeping staff manager at FBI Headquarters @ 7pm, tonight. Say you're there for the **night shift**.

If you decide to go to FBI Headquarters as instructed, go to **page 59**.

If you decide that you aren't ready, go to **page 62**.

You are excited about your mission and decide to **report to** the FBI as Betty has asked. Now the mission is the **real deal**—there is **no turning back**.

During dinner, Cat continues to be **nosy**. She asks about your past and your history with Nick. You are very careful about what you say. It is exhausting trying to **keep your story straight.** When dinner is over, you lie down on the couch and close your eyes. But Cat won't **take a hint.**

"Do you mind? I want to update my Facebook page," she says. Before you can refuse, Cat takes out her phone and bends down next to you. Out **of the blue,** she **snaps a photo.**

"I'm not so sure that's a good idea," you say, frowning and turning away.

She takes another picture. "Oh, oops," she says with a knowing smile.

Over her shoulder, you see her phone. The picture of you on the screen is unflattering. Your eyes are **bloodshot,** and your hair is messy. Part of your face is blocked by your raised hand. Next to you in the shot, Cat looks as flawless as usual, not a **hair out of place**.

"**Come on.** Don't post it," you beg. You are getting more and more annoyed with Cat's **pushy** attitude. "I look awful."

"But I love it," she says, pouting. "Now I have my **selfie** memento with you."

She looks triumphant, as if she has just **bagged** a hunting trophy. You have no idea why she would care so much about a photo of you. Being her flirtatious self, she **blows you a kiss**. You are too tired to **put up a fight** and merely shrug back.

Nick comes home at around eleven o'clock. Although it is late, you are happy to have someone around to distract Cat.

"Did you miss me?" he asks.

Cat greets him and kisses his cheek. You open your eyes and try to look uninterested. Nick walks over to you on the couch. As a greeting, he sits on your head.

"Get off me!" you yell, pushing his butt away from your face. You are still feeling annoyed from your experience with Cat earlier. Nick's behavior now isn't helping.

"He's **alive and kicking**," Nick declares as he jumps on top of you and wrestles you from the couch to the floor. You try to escape, but he is too strong now. You used to be an **equal match** as kids. "**Give up** yet, Kiddo?"

You try to pretend he didn't call you Kiddo again, but of course Cat notices.

"Why do you always treat Kevin like your little brother?" Cat asks from the kitchen as she makes Nick a plate of spaghetti. "**Come on**, leave him alone and have some dinner."

Later that night, after Cat goes into the bedroom, Nick sits beside you on the couch. "Hey, Kiddo—agh! I keep calling you that. Sorry, it's a **hard habit to break**."

"**Tell me about it**," you answer. "Cat could **catch on**."

"Listen, I know I've been **out of left field** lately. I guess my mind has been preoccupied. That's why it might seem like I've been avoiding you. I have responsibilities now. I can't just **blow off** work; they depend on me. Also, my window washing business is really starting to **pick up**. I need to start thinking about the future."

"The future?"

"Yeah. Buying a ring, starting a family . . . "

Did he just say he wants to buy a ring?

"And then what happened with your mother just came **out of the blue**. It was **bad timing**. That's why I'm so glad you were able to come here. **Don't get me wrong**; I'm worried about her. She's always been like a mother to me. I'm hoping for a **big break** in the case soon."

You nod with understanding. At least Nick has **cleared the air** about his lack of involvement. It sounds like his **hands are tied** with work. For all his faults, you do admire Nick's strong work ethic. You just wish he would be more sensitive about your feelings.

"You forgive me?" Nick asks. "Oh, and what do you think of Cat?"

You give him a strange look. Nick has never been one to ask for forgiveness. And Cat—what does any of this have to do with her?

"She's great, I guess," you say slowly and then add, "As long as your girlfriend isn't trying to **pull the wool over our eyes**."

Nick pauses and then **belts out** the loudest laugh you have ever heard, slapping you hard on the back.

"I'm serious," you say.

"Wow, something has really gotten **under your skin**," he says, peering at you in surprise.

If you think that Nick is saying that the case is bothering you, go to **page 56**.

If you think that Nick is saying that Cat has been irritating you, go to **page 58**.

Nick is saying that the case is bothering you. Yes, it is true . . . but it is also true that you have your **eye on** Cat. Some of the things she does might be related to your mother's disappearance. You don't have any hard evidence, of course, **just a feeling**.

Lowering your voice, you try to explain this to Nick. "You should have seen how she gave me the **third degree** earlier. Cat doesn't miss a thing. She already notices how you treat me like a little brother. Recently, she's been trying to post photos of me on Facebook. It's weird. Worst of all, I think she's been following me."

Nick **brushes you off**. "Even if she did notice **something was up**, would it be **a big deal**? Listen, you don't have to worry about her. Everything's cool, I promise. She's a good woman, Kiddo. I trust her." He pauses and **looks you in the eye**. "In fact, I love her."

You don't have to be a detective to know that much.

"It's only been—"

"A whole month! That's the longest I've ever been in a relationship. Besides, Kiddo, **when you know, you just know**."

Nick reaches into his pocket to show you something. "I was going to surprise you . . . I think I'm going to **propose** to Cat soon." He hands you a silver ring with a green stone that looks strangely familiar. "It was your mother's," he explains.

You inspect it and notice a Mayan symbol carved in the jade stone. A **flood of memories** comes back to you. You know the ring is valuable and meant a lot to your mother. Your mother might love Nick, but you find it hard to believe she would give the ring to your cousin.

"Mother gave that to you?" Your stomach twists into knots. "That ring is special, Nick. It was meant to **stay in the family**. Are you sure you really know this woman?"

You glance nervously at the bedroom door. Could Cat be listening?

"Of course I'm sure! We know everything about each other."

"Yeah, um, except that I'm your cousin, who is here because your aunt was kidnapped, and we're trying to find her."

"Well, yeah, *that*," Nick admits. "I do feel bad keeping a secret like that from her. Are you sure we can't tell her about it? It would be a relief to stop pretending."

You shake your head. "Bad idea."

He nods silently. You feel terrible about keeping secrets from Nick—and asking him to do the same with Cat. But as Betty has said, it is for his own protection.

"Well, I do have some good news to share . . . " you start to say, **changing the subject**.

"A **lead** on Ana?" He looks at you with hope.

You **put on your best face**. "Not quite. I received a message from her coworker. She said the police are doing a good job and have some information."

"Really? I thought the police were **stuck**. Plus, what about what Ana said on the phone—that you could help in some way?"

"I'll stay here until they find her. The police want me to come in sometime soon for more interviews anyway."

Nick looks worried. "What if they don't find her?"

Then, I will.

"Don't worry," you say, patting Nick on the back. "They will."

Go to **page 59**.

Nick is saying that Cat has been irritating you. "She sometimes makes me feel uncomfortable, but Cat's not **getting under my skin**."

"What's bothering you then?"

"Honestly, I don't feel like you're being very supportive. All you ever do is talk about Cat."

"But what can I do? I'm no expert. I already told the police everything I know. I just feel like I need to stay out of the way and **keep my mouth shut**. It's hard enough trying to keep this situation from my girlfriend." Nick crosses his arms and looks at you accusingly. "The real problem, I think, is you."

"Me?"

"You're living in a **make-believe** world, a fantasy world. You're living through your crime novels—being secretive and suspicious of everyone. But this is reality. **Face it**, Kiddo. You're letting this investigation **go to your head**."

Now you are hurt. Is he right? Are your books and movies influencing you too much? No, you refuse to believe it. Nick is the one living in a fantasy world, believing that a beautiful actress is actually **in love** with him. You want to give him a **piece of your mind** but stay quiet and calm.

"Besides," he adds, his voice softening, "I care about you. I'd hate for something bad to happen to you. You've got a **bright future**. You're going to be **bigger than any** Sherlock Holmes."

"Look, I can't ignore it when I start having doubts. With Cat, sometimes I wonder. Don't you think she **lays it on too thick**?"

"What do you mean?" Nick says, his voice hardening.

"Don't you ever get the feeling she's . . . just acting?"

Nick ignores your accusation. "Cat's just a normal person. **Nosey**, maybe. But you make her sound like **Pussy Galore** from *James Bond*." He looks at you with pity. "See a pattern? You're letting this case **get under your skin**."

Go to **page 56**.

[CHAPTER THREE]

~ Getting Your Feet Wet

YOU ARRIVE AT FBI Headquarters as instructed. Standing in the shadow of the large, impressive building, you almost turn back. But you have **spent the day** putting aside your doubts. After **getting your feet wet** with this first mission, you hope the experience will prepare you to **take on** more missions.

Calmly you walk inside. A big man in a security uniform sits behind a desk by the elevators. He looks **bored** as he gazes at the **footage** from several cameras at different locations in the building. "This way, sir," he says, gesturing for you to come to the desk. His eyes never leave the screens.

"Good evening. I work for housekeeping," you say confidently.

"Do you have your ID?"

Of course I'd need an ID to enter the FBI Headquarters! But Betty never gave me an ID.

You pat your pockets. "I think I forgot mine tonight."

He finally **makes eye contact**. "Well then, you're not working tonight," he says, indifferent.

"I—I'm sorry, sir," you say. "It's my first day. If I don't show up, they'll **fire** me. Can't you **make an exception**?"

He shakes his head. "First day? More reason you should have your ID. This is the FBI. We don't make exceptions."

Unsure what to do next, you walk back toward the entrance. You can't believe you are failing at your mission already. How will you get past the guard? Outside, you notice a woman sweeping the walkway right in front of the revolving doors.

"Excuse me," you say, hoping she will **move out of the way**.

Instead of stepping aside, she **stands firm**, looking at the ground intently where she sweeps. You remember Betty's tip about the signal and start counting. Sure enough, the woman does three short sweeps and then three long sweeps.

"Are you working tonight?" she asks, looking at you like you have been coworkers for a long time.

"I am," you answer, looking back inside at the big man at the front desk. "But I forgot my ID. I can't go in."

"That's because you dropped it here the other night." She takes out an official **ID badge** with your picture on it. "I found it." You look at your own picture in amazement. It has been **altered**, but you recognize it from your Facebook account.

"Oh, yeah," you say, trying to sound natural. "I'm so careless sometimes." You turn to go back to the entrance again.

"Wait," the woman says. "One more thing . . . " She hands you a key that you put in your pocket. "Office #3 on the third floor is very dirty. It hasn't been cleaned since the employee took some **time off—family leave**, I think. Might be a good place to start cleaning."

The woman **tilts her head** and waits for you to respond. "Office #3," you repeat back.

"Have a great first day," the woman says as she continues sweeping the sidewalk.

Back at the security desk, you present your badge to the guard. You wonder if he can hear your **heart pounding** in your chest. "Got lucky. My coworker found my badge on the ground. I think I dropped it during my shift the other day."

The man examines the ID badge and looks at you suspiciously. "I thought you said you were new."

*I really need some practice **getting my story straight***. "Yeah, I am," you start to say, "but, uh, I've only been here a few times . . . for new hire training."

The guard looks at you again strangely before he **runs** your badge through a machine. The machine beeps, and he hands it back to you, satisfied. He nods toward the elevators. "Use the elevators to your left. Housekeeping is working on the third floor right now."

When you get to the third floor, you see a man and woman in housekeeping uniforms. The woman is vacuuming the carpet, and the man is pushing a large trashcan on wheels. Since they aren't sweeping, you don't know if they are regular workers or Cleaning House agents. As you try to **get your sense of direction**, the woman **looks up** and turns off the vacuum cleaner.

"Who are you?" she asks **point-blank**.

Nervous, you show her your badge. "I was sent here to clean by—" you stop to glance at your ID badge "—Capital Cleaners. New account. And you are?"

"Jules," she says gruffly. "I'm the manager tonight." She looks you up and down, **sizing you up**. "I didn't know we were getting a third person. We don't need an extra **pair of hands**."

"Well, I was told to come here," you say, shrugging. "First day."

Jules grumbles softly and **rolls her eyes**. She looks over at Mani, who is busy emptying small trashcans into a larger one, and whistles. "We got us a **newbie** here reporting for **boot camp**. **Show him the ropes** tonight, will you?"

If you think that Jules is asking Mani to tie you up and get rid of you, go to **page 89**.

If you think that Jules is asking Mani to teach you how to do the job, go to **page 92**.

You aren't ready yet—not even close. While you are flattered that Betty has so much confidence and **faith in you**, you still think you need at least some training before you **get your feet wet**. If you are unprepared, you will likely **blow the mission**, or worse—put yourself or others in danger. With more knowledge about the **ins and outs** of going undercover, you can better help Cleaning House, well, **clean house**.

Your thumb is **poised** to type your response to Betty when Cat appears, **hovering over you** on the couch. "Morning, **Sleepy Head**," she says. She is holding a tray of bacon that smells delicious. "Did you sleep well?"

Cat doesn't leave me alone for a second.

You put your smartphone **face down** on the table without finishing your message and nod nervously.

"Breakfast?"

You nod again, this time with more enthusiasm. You never did eat that eggplant last night.

"I'll **fix you a plate** of bacon and eggs. And I swear I won't burn it this time."

While Cat is busy in the kitchen, you **pick up** your phone again and respond to Betty.

Best to get training first before the mission.

In a few seconds, she sends back a message.

Meet me at my office 1400 K St #101, @ 9am, today.

"Where's Nick?" you ask Cat.

"You missed him. He already left for work, of course," Cat says, handing you a plate of eggs and bacon piled high. "He tried to wake you up, but you were **sound asleep**."

You aren't so sure about that. You are a pretty **light sleeper**, especially now that your **nerves are shot**. Didn't Nick say that you would **catch up** in the morning? The truth is you are starting to think that he is avoiding you **on purpose**.

You look at the time on your phone. It is already eight o'clock, and you aren't sure exactly how far away Betty's office is. You quickly finish your breakfast, get ready, and **head out**.

Go to **page 64**.

You arrive at 1400 K Street at nine o'clock **sharp**. Betty meets you at the security desk. She looks taller than you remember her at the Laundromat, and her handshake is even firmer.

"Thank you for coming on such **short notice**," she says to you in a professional voice. It feels as if you are meeting for the first time. "Please follow me, and we'll **get down to business**."

Nervous, you follow Betty around the corner to office #101, trying to **read her face** about what to expect at your first training.

"I think this was a good decision," she says as she unlocks her office door. "You're **in good hands**. I'll do my best to teach you everything you need to know in the **short time** that we have."

She motions for you to **sit down** in a leather chair that **faces** a desk cluttered with computers, cell phones, tablets, and piles of papers, photos, and newspaper clippings. Your **heart leaps with excitement**. It is as if you have just **stepped into** one of your favorite crime novels.

"Lesson one in being a good undercover detective," Betty begins, **taking a seat** at her desk, "is learning how to **spot** when someone is lying or keeping information from you."

You nod. You are **in awe** of this woman.

"People might lie with their words, but their faces and **body language** always tell the truth. For example, they might pause, fidget, stutter, scratch their nose, or **pull back** or **look away** for just a **split second**. They do all these things without even knowing it. It's beyond their control." She pauses and looks at you for a reaction.

You swallow and try to maintain **eye contact**. Why do you suddenly feel nervous when you have nothing to hide? You wonder if she is trying to **read your body language** right now.

"Uh, sounds pretty easy to **figure out**, then," you say.

"Usually," Betty responds. "Unless the person you are dealing with is a professional—like Foster or someone working for Foster. Then, it becomes more difficult. Especially when you are nervous or uncertain yourself."

You understand what she is trying to say. You need to have more confidence if you are going to **go undercover**.

"Detectives must be trained to detect lies in other people, usually by looking at the tiny details—we call them 'micro-expressions.' We find these facial clues by first studying someone while they are communicating normally—we call that our '**baseline**.'" She pauses to pull out her smartphone and starts recording you on video. "Let me show you what I mean."

You feel yourself sweat. Betty chuckles softly and reassures you. "Hey, don't worry. This is the easy part. You're just going to tell me the truth. That's it. I'm going to ask you some simple or obvious questions about yourself that we both know are true. **No matter what**, I want you to answer naturally, without even thinking about it. Got it?"

Easier said than done, but you nod and agree to the test, knowing it is better to learn this now than when you are **face-to-face** with a suspect.

"Besides, this is just for training purposes and to get you comfortable."

You nod again.

"Here we go." Betty **clears her throat**. "What's your name?"

"David."

"How old are you, David?"

"Twenty-two."

"What's your mother's name?"

"Ana."

Suddenly, her voice changes. Her easygoing expression is gone. "Did Ana give you that watch?"

"Yes."

"Are you sure?" Her voice is more urgent, louder.

"Yes."

"Is there any special significance to the watch?"

You pause for a second, **taken aback** by the question. "No—"

"No?" Betty seems surprised.

"Well, it's personal, of course," you explain. "My mother gave it to me when I turned eighteen. She said she wanted me to think of her whenever I looked at it, to remind me that one day, **when the time was right,** we'd be together again." You try to keep your voice calm. "Other than that, I don't think it has any other significance."

"Is that all she said about the watch?"

You feel yourself blush. You know this should be easy, but you pushed so many memories of your mother **out of your mind** because they were so painful. "Honestly, I can't remember. It was a while ago."

"Are you sure you don't know anything else?"

"Anything else?" You frown. You told her the truth, but she doesn't seem to believe you now. In fact, it **sounds like** she is trying to **trip you up**.

"You never thought that your mother was giving you a secret message?" Betty asks. There is a whiff of desperation in her voice.

"A secret message?" you repeat back. Your **mouth is dry**.

"Just answer the question."

You **think hard**, trying to remember the day your mother called you on your eighteenth birthday. That was the year she brought Nick to the U.S. instead of you. The watch became your **consolation prize**. You were very angry.

"One day you'll understand. **When the time is right** ..." your mother said on the phone that day.

"Understand what?" you answered bitterly. "That you **couldn't care less** about me?"

"Happy Birthday, son," she replied sadly. "I wish I could be there with you. **There's no place like home**."

"No," you finally say, **waking up** from your daydream. "My mother never gave me a secret message. The watch was just a gift."

"Are you sure?"

"Yes," you say more forcefully.

Then a **chilling thought** occurs to you: *Could I be one of Betty's prime suspects?*

Betty quickly smiles and **turns off** the video camera. She seems satisfied. "You did very well, David. I'm sorry if I made you feel uneasy. I wanted to study your facial expressions when you were **under pressure**."

You sigh with relief. Betty is just trying to make sure you have the confidence to go undercover. You nod and try to relax as you continue the **rest of** the training.

After a lunch break, Betty explains that the second part of the training involves analyzing hours of video from suspects that Cleaning House has interviewed **over the years** for different cases. For the rest of the day and into the evening, Betty shows you video footage of suspects and teaches you how to identify signs that they are lying. After that, you practice roleplaying in which you are the "suspect," and she shows you how to relax your face and body, to avoid making those signs yourself. You realize that **going undercover** involves a lot of lying and pretending, almost like being an actor in a play or movie.

More hours pass. Although you are exhausted at the end of the training, you start to feel more confident about your detective skills. You aren't the only one who notices.

"You're **a natural**," Betty says, impressed. "You have a real instinct for this kind of work."

"I guess I **get it** from my mother," you answer with a shrug.

"I think you've got a good foundation now." She looks around her desk. "Anyway, it's getting late, and I have a lot of work to finish up. We'll end here. But I'll be sending you a message later about where to go next. I'm thinking the first step is to identify key people who may know Foster, or try to find out where he was last."

You nod and smile. You are grateful. The training sessions were uncomfortable but exciting. You thank Betty for the experience, but your enthusiasm seems to worry her more.

"Listen, most detectives have to go through months and sometimes years of extensive training before they are given a mission. Don't **get ahead of yourself**. Today was just a **crash course**."

"There's more?"

"I'll still need to **keep an eye on you** just **in case** you get into trouble."

"What do you mean?"

From her desk drawer, Betty pulls out a tiny toolkit. "Give me your watch, please."

Why is everyone so interested in my watch?

Reluctantly, you **take off** your watch and **hand it over**. She opens the glass cover with a metal pin. Skillfully, she examines the inside of the watch as if looking for something, and then she shakes her head.

Of course there's nothing inside my watch. What did she expect?

With her other hand, Betty shows you a small **microchip**. "It's a **tracking device**," she explains, planting the chip inside your watch. "We'll use it to track your every move. No matter where you are, one of our agents will be nearby. See this tiny button on the side of the watch? If you're ever in danger or feel threatened, push it. It will **turn on** a signal in the device and—" she snaps her fingers "—we'll be there in minutes."

You take back the watch and strap it securely to your wrist.

"No more phone calls. When we get a new **lead** about Foster or your mother, we'll send you a clue through Facebook about where to go next."

You think about the strange blocked phone call at Nick's apartment. Was that Betty? You want to ask her about it, but she continues with her instructions. Betty isn't the kind of person you interrupt so easily.

"Our tech people customized your Facebook account. The security settings we installed will make sure no one can **hack** your messages except us. Any questions?"

You look back at your watch. "How will I know who is **on my side**—who the, er, good guys are?"

"Good question. We have a special **signal** we use at Cleaning House, Inc. It goes like this: three short sweeps, three long sweeps." Betty grabs a broom from the closet and shows you the exact sweeping motion. It is the same action you saw her do with the mop when you walked into the Laundromat.

You feel anxious to get started. "Thank you so much for everything," you say again.

Betty nods. "I'm sure we'll find your mother in **no time**."

It is hard to believe that just a few days ago you were under the **false impression** that your mother was just a cleaning lady. There is so much more to her story now.

When you get up to leave, you glance down at Betty's desk. You notice scattered photos spread across the table. While most of them are pictures of nameless men and women who are probably all suspects in different cases, you think you see one photo with a familiar face.

"Hey, can I see that?" you ask, pointing at the photo.

Betty covers the photos on her desk with her hands, blocking them from view. "I really have a lot of work to do, so . . . " Then, noticing your hesitation, she adds, "We **don't leave any stone unturned**. To a good detective, everyone is a suspect—and I mean *everyone*—even those **closest to us**."

If you think that Betty is saying that everyone is a suspect—even your friends and family, go to **page 70**.

If you think that Betty is saying that everyone is a suspect—even you, go to **page 72**.

Betty is saying that everyone is a suspect—even your friends and family. **A shiver runs down your spine**. You are pretty sure that you saw Nick's photo on Betty's desk.

My own cousin? Is that why Betty didn't want him involved?

Your **mind is reeling**. You think about how strange Nick has been acting and how he sounded when he called you. And since you arrived in D.C., he hasn't been trying that hard to help you find your mother. But **deep down inside**, you know it isn't **the whole picture**. That is why you decided to **take matters into your own hands** and show some initiative. Betty's training might have worked a little too well.

In your hand is an envelope you **nicked** from Betty's desk while she was installing the tracking device on your watch. With all the clutter on her desk, it will take Betty a while before she notices anything is missing.

You think about all the crime novels you have read. *I've got my own **tricks up my sleeve**.*

On the way to the bus stop, you glance briefly at the front of the envelope.

Frederick Foster

But this information isn't even the most interesting thing. The name is written in your mother's handwriting—at least, you think it is. You are about to look inside the envelope when you hear the bus approaching. Quickly, you put the envelope back in your jacket pocket for safekeeping and pull out your wallet instead. As you are **counting change** for the fare, someone runs into you from behind.

"**Watch it!**" you say defensively.

You **turn around** to see an unshaven man in a black hooded coat waving what looks like a paper bag at you. He smells of liquor and cigarettes. Before staggering away down the sidewalk, he mumbles something you can't quite hear.

You feel for your wallet. *Phew.* It is still there, **safe and sound**.

On the bus, you reach for the envelope you tucked away in your jacket pocket. You are eager to see what is inside. Frederick Foster's name was on the outside, and it was written in handwriting that might belong to your mother. She wrote it, or someone forged it to fool Betty. What could it all mean? Maybe you will finally have some information to prove to Betty that you can handle this mission on your own.

Nothing.

All you can feel with your hand is the smooth lining of your jacket. You **take off** the jacket and shake it. You check all the pockets again. Frantic, you try the back pocket of your jeans and inside your shirt.

The envelope is gone.

Did you drop it somewhere on the street or on the bus? Was someone following you? You shake your head. The only thing **out of the ordinary** was the drunk man who bumped into you at the bus stop.

*No doubt about it now—I've **been had**.*

A question remains: Who does that guy work for?

You decide to **take a quick detour** and get off the bus early to **walk off** your worries. It is late in the evening by the time you return to Nick's apartment.

Go to **page 134**.

Betty is saying that everyone is a suspect—even you. Although the photo you saw on her desk was blurry, you are confident it was your own face staring back at you. "**Leave no stone unturned**," she warned. She must be considering all possibilities. But how can Betty believe *you* are a suspect in your own mother's disappearance, while at the same time trusting you to **go undercover** to save her?

You **look down** at your watch. *Is that why she put the **tracking device** on me?* She wants to know your every move, to **keep an eye on you** because she suspects you of something—but what? It doesn't **add up**.

*Betty must know what she's doing. This is all **bigger than me**.*

You decide that the best thing to do is to go home and get some rest and prepare for your first mission.

Go to **page 73**.

The next morning, you **wake up** to a message from Betty.

A professor of Ancient Mesoamerican Culture at American University named Dr. Khan claims to have talked to your mother on the night she disappeared. Attend her class tonight @ 6pm to see what you can **dig up**.

This should be fairly easy. You already have some basic knowledge about Mesoamerican cultures and some fluency in reading Mayan hieroglyphs—thanks to your mother and the copy of a Mayan codex she kept.

For the rest of the day, you **go over** the detective skills Betty taught you the day before. Interviewing and lie detection should **come in handy** when you speak to Dr. Khan. You also get online to find out about the professor and her class, but **nothing out of the ordinary** comes up in your search. At five o'clock, you take the bus to the other side of the city to American University. When you arrive on campus, you stop to look at a directory and map.

"Psst," a voice says from behind you.

A man in a cleaning uniform sweeping up cigarette butts on the sidewalk approaches you. You look at him warily.

"Drop this?" He points to a book bag on the grass in front of the Liberal Arts building.

You shake your head. "It isn't mine."

"Are you sure?" he asks again. He takes his broom and starts sweeping: three short sweeps, three long sweeps.

"Uh, I mean, yes," you say, recognizing the Cleaning House signal. You take the book bag when he hands it to you.

"Thought so," he says with a wink. "Everything you need for class is in there. Don't be late."

You open the book bag and find a class schedule, student ID badge with your picture on it, a book on Mesoamerican culture, and a baseball cap. You **put on** the baseball cap and go to the room number on your class schedule.

By the time you get to the room, class has already started. You scan the classroom, a large auditorium with fifteen or twenty rows of seats. You sneak into the back, **sit down**, open your book bag, and set the textbook on the table in front of you.

"You make an important point, Stephanie," Dr. Khan is saying to a student with striking red hair sitting in the front row. Up on the large projector screen is the image of a Native American **deity** in the form of a jaguar. Dr. Khan pauses for a moment, **makes eye contact** with you briefly, and continues her lecture.

At the end of class when the students are dismissed, you aren't sure what to do next, so you sit there, waiting for the professor to notice you.

"May I help you?" asks Dr. Khan, walking toward you after everyone else has left. She is a tiny woman in a black turtleneck sweater. She wears big, thick glasses that make her look owlish.

"I have a quick question about the function of deities in Mayan culture, Dr. Khan," you lie. Luckily, you have a lot of experience being a confused student at your own university.

"Sure. Come to my office hours on Mondays and Wednesdays, from three to four." She turns away, and then **whips** around. "I've never seen you before in class. Are you sure you're registered?"

You aren't sure what to do next. Feeling awkward, you decide to gather your things. Then you stop. A Post-It note is stuck to the inside cover of your textbook.

Tell Khan you're here to clean house.

You **clear your throat** to get Dr. Khan's attention again. "Ahem," you cough. "Actually, I'm here to **clean house**."

Dr. Khan **stops in her tracks**. She turns around and looks at you, adjusting her glasses, as if you have finally **come into focus**.

"So you're Ana's son," she says, **sizing you up**. "They told me you might be coming. Nice disguise. You **fit in**. This way, please. We'll talk in my office."

You follow her down the hall to a cluttered room. Shelves upon shelves in the office are filled with Mesoamerican art. "What can I do for you?" she asks when you follow her inside.

You close the door behind you and decide to **cut to the chase**. "I'll be direct, Dr. Khan. I was told you were the last person to see my mother the night she disappeared. I was wondering if you had any information about that night that might help me find her."

"Let me think . . . " she begins, motioning for you to **take a seat**. "I believe I saw her around half past ten. That's usually when she comes to my office to clean. I remember I was working late, analyzing some new **artifacts** that had been **excavated** from Tikal in Guatemala. The objects had Mayan hieroglyphs on them. Your mother liked to look at them and often asked me questions."

"I'm not surprised. It was a big interest of hers. My mother had a copy of a Mayan codex."

"Indeed?"

Dr. Khan settles into her leather chair behind her desk. The chair makes her look smaller but no less intimidating. Behind her, you notice a large, hand-woven tapestry of a stone temple. It frames her body perfectly. You try to hide your growing nervousness.

"Very interesting, indeed," she continues, **drumming her fingers** on the desk. "Was there any special symbol from the codex that you two liked to use to communicate with each other?"

"Huh?"

"I assume Ana taught you how to read them—the hieroglyphics."

You nod uneasily. Her directness and questions are starting to make you feel queasy. Once again, just like during your training with Betty, you feel that you are the one **being grilled** and put **under the microscope**.

"I'm not sure where you're going with this."

Dr. Khan holds up a small artifact that looks like some sort of tool with a carved mark on it. "How about this symbol? Does it **ring a bell**? Does it possibly mean anything to you?"

You glance at it briefly but feel distracted. This investigation is going nowhere. You need more details about that night before your mother disappeared.

"Something about family, I think," you mumble. Then, leaning forward, you say firmly, "Listen, Dr. Khan, I'd love to chat more about Mayan stuff, but I don't have much time. It's important you tell me anything you remember that night. Was there any indication my mother was in trouble or under pressure?"

"Of course, of course," Dr. Khan says apologetically. "Back to the issue **at hand**." Dr. Khan stares thoughtfully at the ceiling. "That night, your mother seemed distracted. Her eyes kept searching around my office—the ceiling, the floors, the closet—like she was looking for something."

"What do you think she was looking for?"

She stops and peers at you intently. Her eyes are big and unblinking behind her thick glasses. "Good question." She shifts in her seat and pauses before she asks, "What do *you* think she could have been looking for?"

There is a hint of accusation in her voice that you don't like. You shrug. "No idea."

But you do have an idea. According to Betty, Foster isn't just looking for his daughter; he is also looking for the fortune that his wife and daughter **ran away** with. Your mind **makes a connection**. *Could this mean Mom might have it? If she does, she might have been looking for a place to hide the fortune, maybe even here in Dr. Khan's office.*

"I see. Fine." Dr. Khan sits back in her chair as if frustrated. "Ana also asked me what time I'd be leaving my office so that she could come back to clean more thoroughly. That was strange because she has cleaned while I've been in my office, and it was never a problem until then." She stares at you hard. "So far, I haven't found any of my artifacts to be missing, but if I do . . . "

Now you understand what Dr. Khan is **getting at**. She thinks your mother was snooping around, looking for something to steal. The professor has a **bone to pick** and she is **taking it out on you**.

"My mother isn't a thief," you say flatly.

Dr. Khan's stare is steady. "Are you sure that's not the reason your mother is missing **in the first place**? Are you sure your mother isn't *hiding* something?"

You can't believe that Dr. Khan would be so quick to accuse your mother of stealing, especially when nothing is even missing. Maybe she is **pushing your buttons** for a reason. But why?

Dr. Khan's smug expression is starting to **piss you off**. You have to leave now before you will say something you regret. You **stand up** and abruptly walk to the door.

"Thank you very much for your time, Dr. Khan."

"Wait. There's something else—"

But you **don't bother** waiting to hear what she has to say. You stride through the darkened hall and down the stairs to the entrance of the building. The campus feels deserted and empty now; few students roam the grounds.

You think about the wasted time you spent with Dr. Khan. You can't believe that Betty said Dr. Khan would be a **promising lead**. The meeting didn't go well at all. Suddenly, you feel a **stab of uncertainty**. Has something important **slipped under your radar**?

If you think that Dr. Khan is hiding something, go to **page 78**.

If you think that your mother was trying to hide something in Dr. Khan's office, go to **page 81**.

Dr. Khan is hiding something. Anyone else would have **jumped to the conclusion** that Dr. Khan was just a rude person—and left it at that. But you have been **raised on a steady diet** of crime novels, puzzles, and detective stories. The questions you have only lead to more. There is something **shady** about her.

While you wait at the bus stop, you think about what you know. Your **gut tells you** that Dr. Khan can't be trusted. She seemed extremely interested in your ability to read Mayan codes. Too interested. She invited you to her office **under false pretenses**. Dr. Khan was **fishing** for something. The question is—what?

Other than you mother's Mayan codex, there really isn't anything related to ancient cultures in your life. In fact, your mother hasn't mentioned anything about codes since you were a kid. She moved to the U.S., and you outgrew the old puzzle games from your childhood—**end of story**. Anyway, why would Dr. Khan ask about Mayan symbols **in the first place**? How are ancient hieroglyphics related to Frederick Foster?

You look down at your hands. Before you stormed out of her office, you took something. It was an impulsive and risky thing to do, but you did it. While Dr. Khan was distracted, you **swiped** a piece of mail from her desk.

You smile to yourself. You couldn't resist. On the front of the envelope was a familiar name.

Frederick Foster

You decided to **seize the day** and act. Sometimes a good detective has to **get his hands dirty**—an important lesson that you have learned from Betty.

Inside the envelope are several folded notes and pieces of paper that could be vital clues. You reach in and remove a business card. Printed in the front is a name: "Franklin Oz, Senior Computer Analyst." It isn't a name you recognize.

Could this be Foster's alias?

You also find an old, faded photograph. In the picture is a man with a prominent mustache. He stands next to a young girl dressed up in a costume—a blue and white, checkered dress. The girl has painted rosy cheeks, freckles, and braided **pigtails**. On her feet are red shoes covered in sequins and glitter. They sparkle in the light. She is also carrying a basket with a toy dog. On the faces of the man and young girl are huge smiles.

You are about to **dig around** some more when you hear the bus approaching. You put the envelope in your jacket pocket for safekeeping and pull out your wallet instead. As you are **counting your change** for the bus fare, a person on a bicycle zooms by and nearly **runs you over**.

"Slow down, buddy," you warn.

The cyclist doesn't even acknowledge you. He is an unshaven man in a black hooded coat carrying a crumpled paper bag. The scent of booze is strong on him.

A woman sitting with you at the bus stop advises you to check your wallet. "**Pickpockets**—you can never be too careful these days," she says sympathetically.

"Good idea." You feel your pocket for your wallet and keys. "Still there."

*The man was so **wasted** that he probably didn't even see me.*

On the bus ride home, you reach for the envelope you tucked away in your jacket pocket. You are eager to see what else is inside. Maybe you will finally have some information to prove to Betty that you can **handle** this mission on your own. You are eager to impress her and **prove yourself**.

But your pocket is empty. *Oh no.*

You **take off** your jacket and shake it. Frantic, you check the back pocket of your jeans and inside your shirt, **just in case** it slipped out.

Nothing.

It is gone. You lost the envelope—and all the clues inside it.

What happened? Could that cyclist have taken it from me?

You are devastated. You decide to send Betty a quick report about the mission. She writes back and reassures you that the mission at American University wasn't a **total washout**.

> Interesting findings. I think we can assume F is using the 'Oz' identity as his **cover**. But we need more information about the little girl in the photograph. It could be crucial. Go home and wait for your next mission.

Go to **page 103**.

Your mother was trying to hide something in Dr. Khan's office on the night she disappeared—you are sure of it. According to Dr. Khan, your mother seemed distracted during her shift. An idea **pops in your mind**. Maybe she knew Foster was after her, so she decided to hide something in the professor's office.

You think about everything that Betty has told you about the suspect, Foster. Because of your mother, he lost everything—his daughter, his fortune—and he would probably do anything to get them back, including go after her. Your mother had no choice but to hide whatever she was protecting.

This could be important evidence, and I need to tell Betty.

In your pocket, your smartphone starts ringing. You **pull out** your phone and see that the number is blocked. *Could it be Betty? No, it can't be her; she said no more phone calls.*

It makes you think back again to that strange phone call in Nick's bathroom the other night. You decide to answer it.

"Hello?" you say into the phone, your **heart pounding**.

"Hi, is Ana there?" says a man's voice.

Ana? Is this a prank call?

"Not right now."

"Who is this?"

You can't say who you really are. The caller either thinks the phone number belongs to your mother or knows that you have her phone. "Um . . . I'm her nephew, Nick. May I ask who's calling?"

"This is Ana's landlord, Hector," the voice replies impatiently. "Ana hasn't paid her rent. And she hasn't **picked up** her mail either; it's starting to pile up. I stopped by her apartment today, but no one answered the door. I was calling to check if she's okay."

Strange . . . Why does Hector have this phone number? You got the phone from the taxi driver. You think about what Betty told you. She said that a network of Cleaning House agents would protect you. Was the taxi driver working for Cleaning House? Did he actually give you Ana's phone?

"Yeah, she's just **out of town** and got **held up**," you lie.

"I see." The **edge in his voice** is gone now. He seems to believe you. "Well, she's never been late on her rent, so it's unusual. And there's a pile of mail here for her. She might have some unpaid bills. I don't want her to have any problems. She's always been a reliable tenant."

You **look at** the time on your phone. It is already after eight o'clock, and most offices are already **long closed**. This could be dangerous. Hector could be one of Foster's people. Or he just might have some information about your mother. Should you ask Betty what to do first? You cringe when you think about what she would say if she knew you disobeyed her order about not answering the phone.

You decide to **take a chance**. Besides, Betty is tracking you; if you have any problems, you can push the emergency button.

"Well, I can pay Ana's rent," you say. "Is it too late to come now?"

"No, I'll be at the office for another hour," Hector answers. He gives you the address of the management office. You see on the GPS that it is about a brisk ten-minute walk from Nick's house, and you don't have to take the bus this time. Walking there will also help you get to know the city better—maybe even provide you some clues.

However, as you start walking, you start to regret it. It is **getting dark**. Thunder is rumbling in the distance. Also, the neighborhood doesn't seem very safe. Only a few streetlamps light the streets, and other than the occasional **hoot** from a group of teenagers, it is very quiet. Every car that drives by **makes you jump**. You wonder what Betty would think if she knew what you were doing.

Wait—doesn't she already know? Aren't her people all around you, watching you in the shadows?

When you finally arrive at the address Hector provided, you are relieved. He meets you when you buzz into the building. "Thanks for **making the time** to come," he says. "My accountant has been **getting on my case** about accepting late rent from tenants."

"No problem," you answer, handing him a thick **wad of cash**. Luckily, your friends were generous in lending you enough money for your trip, and you can **cover** your mother's rent. Hector seems stunned that you have been carrying around such a large sum of money, but he doesn't ask questions.

"It's just not like Ana to leave town without paying her rent first."

You watch his face closely, examining his eyes and mouth. You continue the conversation and see how his eyes move. Does he shift his gaze too much? Does he **make eye contact** or **look away**? Eventually, you decide that he is telling the truth. He seems genuinely concerned about your mother.

"Ana's been **under a lot of pressure** at work. She must have forgotten."

He nods with understanding. "She told me."

"Oh?" You try not to sound too surprised.

"I have good relationships with most of my tenants. Ana has lived here for several years now. Sometimes we even do favors for each other. She'd clean for me, while I'd give her rides to run errands. Anyway, I can't imagine how much work it must be to clean houses and offices for a living. I hate cleaning my own house!"

"Do you remember her saying anything **out of the ordinary** about her job lately?"

"Let me think. She just complained about the usual stuff: being tired, her back hurting, clients making demands. Although she did mention something about someone being greedy—**I can't remember exactly**. She said this person would **clean her out** one day. I'm not really sure what she meant by that."

Clean her out? This is different from what Nick and Betty said about possible motives. They said she had aired **someone's dirty laundry** and that caused the person to go after her. You make a **mental note** of this while Hector continues talking.

"Anyway, Ana was mostly just sad about having to be here **in the first place**—you know, since she can't have her son here with her.

I'd often ask her why she couldn't just go visit her son or bring him here, but then she'd **change the subject** and talk about something else."

He reaches behind the mail slots and hands you a pile of envelopes held together by a rubber band. "This is another reason why I called. I know Ana was expecting an important piece of mail."

"Thank you so much, Hector," you say as you take your mother's mail securely in your hands.

You look through the pile, hoping to see something that **stands out**. Most of the envelopes look like utility bills. You notice her address is located on the same street—probably only a few buildings away, in unit #202. Could there be more clues inside her apartment? The police already did **a sweep**, but maybe they missed something.

"So, anything important there?" Hector asks innocently, watching you examine the mail in your hands.

"Not really," you say, flipping through the stack again. Then something **grabs your attention**. You **come across** an envelope addressed to someone else.

Frederick Foster

You slide the piece of mail into your jacket to inspect later. "I think I have what I need," you say, handing Hector the rest of the envelopes. "The rest of these can wait until she comes back."

Loud thunder rattles the building. The lights **flicker** on and off in the lobby.

"Well—I think you'd better get home," Hector says quickly, walking you to the door. "Try to **beat the storm**."

Outside the management office, you breathe a **sigh of relief**. You weren't sure if it was a good idea to meet someone you didn't know without **clearing it first** with Betty, but it has **turned out** to be a good decision—so far. You have some mail addressed to Foster, and you know the address to your mother's apartment now.

Above you, more thunder crackles in the dark sky. You aren't exactly sure how to get back to Nick's apartment from here. You don't like the idea of walking through a bad neighborhood and looking lost. You search for the right direction to go.

"**On second thought**," Hector says, standing with you in the parking lot, "it's late, and the storm is **about to break**. You don't want to **stand out** right now—especially in this neighborhood. I can give you a ride back to your place."

If you think that Hector is saying that you shouldn't be standing or walking around outside during a storm at night, go to **page 86**.

If you think that Hector is saying that you don't want people to know you are a tourist in a bad neighborhood, go to **page 87**.

Hector is saying that you shouldn't be standing or walking around outside during a storm at night. You agree with him. Still, you don't feel completely comfortable getting in a car with someone that you barely know, no matter how nice and genuine he seems to be. You try to think of an excuse.

"You're probably right," you answer him. "I shouldn't **stand out** in the rain. But you've already done enough by letting me **come over**. I think I can just **wait out** the storm in the lobby. Meanwhile, I'll find the closest bus route." You wave your phone at him.

Hector **cocks his head to the side**. "I'm not sure you understand what I mean," he responds with concern. "Robberies and attacks are common in this neighborhood, especially **after dark**. They often target people walking alone or waiting for the bus. The most likely victims are people who don't **look like** they live around here—people who **stand out**."

"So it's obvious that I'm not from **around here**?"

Hector nods and tries to hide his smile. "Well, it's not that you *look* different . . . "

"How do I **stand out**, then?"

"People from **around here** know not to be outside at this hour. We have a lot of tourists in this city, and it's always them who are walking around at night, looking like they don't know where they're going, looking down at their phones and not **paying attention**. You'd be a **sitting duck**."

Go to **page 87**.

Hector is saying that you don't want people to know you are a tourist in a bad neighborhood. You smile. Hector **has a point**. Your mother's landlord seems very genuine and nice, but you don't want to trust him too quickly. You know from Betty's training that anyone could be a suspect. Also, you have the chance to go to your mother's apartment, which is just nearby.

"Thanks, but I don't need a ride," you say.

"**Suit yourself**. Careful out there," Hector cautions. Then you hear several clicks as he locks the front door behind him.

Large raindrops hit your forehead. You **look up** at the sky and realize you probably have a few minutes until it **starts to pour**. You zip up your jacket and jog over to your mother's address. When you get to the building, you find yourself with a group of people running to get inside away from the storm. You rush in through the open lobby doors with the crowd.

The inside of the building is hot and muggy. On the first floor, there is music blaring from several of the ground floor apartments. Kids play and **hang out** in the hallways. You push past them, go up to the second floor, and rush over to #202.

There is no one around on the floor. You rattle the doorknob several times, but it is solidly locked. Then you remember a trick you learned from one of your spy novels. You take your wallet, find a credit card, and slip it against the doorframe. The plastic card bends against the wooden frame.

Sweating from the effort, you unzip your jacket and take it off. The envelope addressed to Foster falls out. You **pick it up** and consider opening it. You **scan** the hallway to make sure you are still alone. Sure that no one else is around, you use one finger to slide open the envelope and **pull out** the contents.

The first thing you find is an old photo. It is faded in color. In the picture is a young man with a mustache. He stands next to a girl who is about ten or eleven years old. She has painted rosy cheeks and freckles and braided **pigtails**. She wears red, glittery shoes and a blue and white, checkered dress. It looks like a costume, maybe of a farm girl. She is also carrying a basket with a little stuffed dog.

You **take a picture** with your smartphone and put the old photo back inside the envelope. Other than the photo, there are also dozens of folded notes inside the envelope. You start to take them out to read them.

Thunk.

You stare at the front door and back away. Were you just hearing things? The sound is clear but faint.

Thunk.

You stop breathing and carefully **plant** your ear against the door. The noise seems to be coming from inside the apartment. You wait and listen again, but you don't hear anything. Is your **mind just playing tricks** on you?

You don't want to **stick around** to find out. In seconds, you are **running down** the stairs. You burst through the lobby doors. Outside, it has already started raining, but you don't care. You are just thankful to be out in the cool air again—away from whoever was inside #202. Using the light from your GPS as a guide, you start jogging home.

If someone was there, did they know I was at the door? What if they are following me now?

You stop and **turn around**. No one is behind you, it seems, but you can't hear or see anything through the heavy rain. Your pace slows to a walk. This time, you hear it. It sounds like the squeak of someone's sneakers on the wet pavement, just a few feet behind you.

Go to **page 107**.

Jules is asking Mani to tie you up and **get rid of** you. After all, Jules doesn't seem too happy about having a new coworker. This isn't **looking good**.

"So, where are these ropes you have to show me?" you ask, half joking. "They're not to tie me up with, I hope."

Mani glares at you for a moment, and then you see the hint of a smile start to form in the corners of his mouth. "You got a strange **sense of humor**, kid." He shoves a broom into your hand. "So how long you been cleanin' offices?"

"Um, for a while now," you lie, keeping your eyes down as you start sweeping in front of you. You don't want him to see how nervous you are.

Mani watches you sweep for a moment and then points and frowns at the ground. "Hey, you **missed a spot**."

"Oh, sorry." You accidentally drop your broom.

He looks at you and sighs. "Listen, you don't have to worry about being **green**. We're not going to get rid of you. We all have to start somewhere, don't we? Everyone deserves a chance. Just **stick with me**. I'll show you how things get done around here quickly and efficiently, so we can all go home **on time**. There's **no place like home**, am I right?"

You nod, handing him back the broom.

"I think I like you," he says. "You look like the kind of guy who'd **do anything for his mother**."

If you think that Mani has discovered who you are and that you are trying to save your mother, go to **page 90**.

If you think that Mani is saying that you are a kind person, go to **page 93**.

Mani has discovered who you are and that you are looking for your mother. He must be an undercover spy working for Foster! But what will you do now? You are alone with him in an empty office building, in the **middle of the night**. You try to **go along with him** as you try to think of a plan.

"Bathrooms are my least favorite," he continues, pointing down the hall, "so you can start there."

As you walk down the hallway, you pass Office #3. You stop to read the nameplate.

FRANKLIN OZ
SENIOR COMPUTER ANALYST

Just as you step closer to get a better look at the name, Mani stops you. "That office is **off-limits**, kid."

"Oh, why?" you ask innocently.

"**Beats me**," he answers, shrugging his shoulders and looking away. "I just do the cleaning around here."

No eye contact. He's lying to me.

Mani hands you a map and a heavy bucket full of soapy water. "If you go straight down, turn right, you'll see the bathrooms. If you need anything, I'll be emptying the trashcans here and on the second floor. Think you can **handle** that on your own?"

You nod, holding the mop tightly in your hands as you walk past him, ready to use it as a weapon if Mani strikes. Instead, Mani **keeps his distance**, whistling cheerfully as he **goes about** his cleaning duties. Maybe you don't have to worry about him after all.

"You know, I think I could get used to having you around," Mani remarks. "Not many people are willing to **take one for the team** like that. At least not without complaining."

"What?"

"Bathroom duty—it's the worst." He cringes at the thought and then gives you a big smile. "And you just volunteered."

You study his expression carefully. Maybe you **got it wrong**. Maybe he doesn't know what you are really here for after all. He looks like a man who is genuinely grateful he is **off the hook** because you are cleaning the bathrooms for him.

Go to **page 93**.

Jules is asking Mani to teach you how to do the job. Mani nods at Jules and makes a motion for you to follow him. "Listen, I got garbage duty," Mani explains, "but I haven't cleaned the toilets yet. You can follow me for a little bit. I'll **show you the ropes** so you can see how everything is done, and then I'll show you where the bathrooms are so you can get started with them."

You follow him from trashcan to trashcan, nodding as you listen to his instructions, but you also look around for Office #3. You continue with him down the row of **cubicles** until you see the number on a door. You read the nameplate.

FRANKLIN OZ
SENIOR COMPUTER ANALYST

You stare at the door, forgetting that Mani is talking to you.

"Got it?" he says, getting your attention again.

"Yeah. It seems easy enough."

He looks in the direction you are staring. "That office was cleaned already. The guy is gone for a while, anyway, so you don't have to worry about that one." He opens the utility closet and pulls out a bucket with cleaning supplies and gloves. "If you go straight down this hallway, turn right, you'll see the bathrooms. I'll be here finishing garbage duty for the next hour. Then, I'll move down to the second floor, and you'll be **on your own**. Can you **handle** that?"

You nod, taking the cleaning supplies from him. He seems relieved not to have bathroom duty.

"**Word of advice**: Just do what I say. If you **mess up**, we all have to stay late. And when I stay late, my wife gets pissed—know what I mean?" He laughs at something. "There's **no place like home**, right?" Mani gives you a smile. "Listen, kid. You seem like a nice guy. Most people don't accept bathroom duty **without a fight**."

Go to **page 93**.

Mani is saying that you are a kind person. You start to feel a little better. For some reason, Mani seems to like and trust you. You walk down the hallway and find the bathrooms. You stop and set the bucket down in front of two doors labeled "Men" and "Women." You know you have to clean the toilets to **keep your cover**, but all you can think about is Franklin Oz's office. How will you get inside #3 without Mani seeing you?

You put your hand in your pocket to make sure the key is still there. You decide you will spend an hour cleaning the bathrooms, waiting until Mani goes down to the second floor, and then you will go back to investigate Office #3.

An hour later, you walk quietly back down the hall and stand against the wall. You look around the corner to see if Mani is anywhere **in sight**. The floor is empty now, and the lights are **dimmed**. You decide he must be downstairs on the second floor by now. Carefully, you take the key out of your pocket and open the office door. The room is dark, and you almost fall over the trashcan by the door. You see it is filled with trash. No one has been in here to clean in weeks.

Mani was lying after all.

You think about **turning on** the lights, but then someone might see you inside the office. You take out your phone and use the light from the screen like a flashlight. Working as fast as you can, you start to look at everything around you, **taking in** all the details. Anything could be a clue for later.

On the wall, there are travel photos of Mr. Oz in exotic places. In several shots, you recognize the pyramids in Egypt and Central America. There is also a framed print of what appears to be a set of Mayan hieroglyphs. On the desk, there is an Elton John CD of "Yellow Brick Road," and an old color photo of a young father standing next to a child who looks like she is dressed in a costume. The girl has bright, pink circles painted on her cheeks, freckles painted on her nose, and braided pigtails. She wears a blue and white, checkered dress. On her feet are red shoes that sparkle. She carries a basket with a toy dog in her arms. You **snap photos** of everything you see.

You try to open the drawers on the desk and cabinets, but they are locked. You nudge the **computer mouse** on the desk to **turn on** the computer. You can't **log on**, but you can see what was on the computer screen before Franklin Oz left: a Facebook page.

For some reason, you can't imagine a serious computer engineer like Oz wasting time on social media. Briefly, you recall Cat's obsession with the social media site. You also think about Betty and how she said Cleaning House had installed security settings onto your Facebook account to prevent other people from hacking it.

You are about to examine the page when you hear a noise outside the door. The rapping sound makes you stop your search. You walk to the closed door and listen. You don't hear anyone on the other side. Slowly, you open the door and step through.

"What were you doing in there?" Mani yells from down the hallway. "That office is **off-limits**." He crosses his arms, waiting for you to speak.

"Yeah, sorry," you say, trying to think of an excuse. "After I finished cleaning the bathrooms, I couldn't find you. When I passed by the office, I thought I heard a noise inside. I went in to see."

Mani scratches his head. "That office is locked."

You **shrug** your shoulders and pretend to be confused. "Actually, the door was unlocked. That's how I got in."

Mani gives you a doubtful look. "What exactly are you trying to **carry out**?"

If you think that Mani is saying that you are trying to steal something from the office, go to **page 95**.

If you think that Mani is saying that you are trying to accomplish a task, go to **page 98**.

Mani is saying that you are trying to steal something from the office. "I wasn't trying to **carry out** anything," you answer defensively. "I'd never take something that wasn't mine."

He looks at you strangely. "Uh-huh."

"I just came in here to make sure everything was okay. But I saw that the trashcan was still full. Do you want me to **carry it out** for you?"

He nods his head. "Fine. Grab it for me."

You go inside Office #3 to get the trashcan. Mani watches **your every move** like a hawk. A few seconds later, the door slams shut behind you, and you hear something click. You run to the door and turn the doorknob, but the door won't open. You have been locked in.

"I'm reporting you!" Mani yells behind the door.

Your **heart races** as you think about what just happened. He must have known you were trying to **carry out** a mission to find evidence inside the office. Mani was probably hired to protect something hidden there. He is working for Foster. You look around. *But protect what?* You already took photos of the things in Oz's office. But if these things were important, would they have been left out for anyone to see?

From the corner of your eye, you see a trashcan. *Of course!*

At first, you don't see anything **out of the ordinary** inside the container, just crumpled pieces of paper and food wrappers. Then you find something that **stands out**: an envelope. You smooth out the envelope with your hands and see a familiar name printed over the address.

Frederick Foster

You are about to open the envelope when you hear excited voices coming from down the hallway. It might be Mani and Jules. What if they are coming back to get rid of the evidence . . . and you?

You stuff the envelope in your back pocket to examine later. You push the emergency button on your watch, hoping that Betty is nearby and that she can find you easily with the tracking device. You look around the room for a way out. The room has a supply closet and two windows. Mani and Jules will certainly find you if you hide in the closet. The only way out is through the windows.

You hear the voices getting closer now. They are almost right outside the office door. Desperately, you open the window and put one leg out on the ledge. Looking down at the street, you realize that if you jump you would break your legs—or worse.

Outside the office door, just a few feet away, Jules and Mani have arrived, their voices loud and angry. Someone is rattling the doorknob. "The lock must be jammed," a voice says.

Your **mind is spinning**. If you get out on the ledge, you might be able to climb down to the second floor. But if you fall, you would certainly injure yourself, maybe even fatally. The last option terrifies you the most though: staying in the office and letting Jules and Mani capture you.

Tires screech on the street below. You look down and see Betty and two men. They jump out and start to unload something from the back—a ladder. They carry the long, heavy ladder and put it right up to the window. **Sucking in** your breath, you climb out the window and **scramble down** the ladder as fast as you can. Betty pulls you into the back of the van and the two men throw the ladder in the back with you. In just a few seconds, the van takes off. Through the back window, you think you can see Mani looking out the third floor window and yelling.

"That was close. We came just **in the nick of time**," Betty exclaims, clapping her hands on the dashboard. Her eyes are **bright with excitement**. "Did you find anything?" she asks you.

You reach inside your pocket for the envelope—but it isn't there. You check all your other pockets and fluff out your clothes, but you still **come up empty-handed**.

"I can't believe it. It's gone. I—I must have lost it." You look helplessly at Betty.

"What's gone?" Betty asks in alarm.

"An envelope I found in Franklin Oz's trash. It was addressed to Frederick Foster."

"Well, you've still confirmed our suspicions," Betty says. "His **cover is blown**. Franklin Oz has to be Frederick Foster."

"There's more," you say, now encouraged by Betty's words. You take out your smartphone and show her all of the photos of the things on his desk. Then you point to the photo of the man next to the little girl in the costume. "His daughter maybe?"

"**Chances are** the little girl is her," Betty agrees. "Too bad it isn't a recent photo. But it does tell us one thing . . . "

You think about the Facebook page left on the computer screen. "He's looking for his daughter," you **blurt out**.

Betty pats you on the back. "You've earned some **time off**. Go home and get some rest. I'll send you details on your next mission tomorrow morning. We need to find out more about Foster's daughter. I think if we can **track down** her down, she'll lead us to Foster somehow."

You smile at her weakly. Although you escaped this time, Mani will surely tell Franklin Oz—Frederick Foster—there is someone after him.

Go to **page 103**.

Mani is saying that you are trying to accomplish a task. Does he suspect you are **carrying out** an undercover mission? You try to think of a good excuse—anything to distract him from suspecting you of doing something sketchy.

"Nothing!" you say. "I wasn't trying to **carry out anything**. I just saw it wasn't clean in there so I thought I'd finish the job—maybe impress you and get some **bonus points**." You smile sheepishly. "I'm sorry it looks like I went against your orders. I did it with the **best of intentions**. Do you want me to go ahead and empty the trashcan for you? **Save you the trouble**?"

"Nah, never mind," Mani answers more calmly.

"Are you sure?"

Mani holds up his hands. "Positive. You know, forget about it. **Water under the bridge** as far as I'm concerned. I'll take care of . . . this situation." He looks around and **takes a deep breath**. His forehead is shiny now with perspiration. "How about you go clean the bathrooms on the second floor now, okay? Impress me with how well you can clean the toilets."

He enters the office and then comes back out with the trashcan, and dumps it into the larger trashcan on wheels. "Well, what are you waiting for, huh?" he asks you as you stand there watching him. "This isn't a Broadway show, rookie. Nothing to see here. Second floor. Bathrooms—go!" He waves his hands to **shoo you away** and then quickly ties up the plastic bag in his cart, even though it isn't even full.

Walking away, you start to worry. Why didn't Mani want you to take out the trash when you were right there? You consider following him to see where he takes the trash, but you know he is already suspicious. If he sees you following him, you won't have any more excuses to give.

On the second floor, you work in the men's bathroom for the rest of the night, staying as far away from Mani as you can. Later, you will think of a way to find the trash he took out.

When the work shift finally ends at three o'clock in the morning, and you see Mani leave for the night, you fill an empty trash bag with wet paper towels. With your bag in hand, you report to the housekeeping manager, Jules.

"How was your first night?" she asks, a little nicer now that the work is finished.

"Good," you say. "I didn't **walk off the job** yet. By the way, where's Mani?"

"Went home for the night. His wife **gets on his case** if he's late," she answers. She hands you a checklist. "Sign this for me, will you?"

"Sure," you say politely. "But I just need to **take care of** one more thing. I think Mani forgot to get rid of this bag of trash from one of the bathrooms. Where should I take it?"

"All the trash from this building goes in the blue trash dumpster behind the building. Take the elevator to the basement level and walk up the steps to the alley. Be careful, though. It's dark there."

Nervous, you take the creaky service elevator down to the basement level. Behind the building, it is very dark and quiet. There are no sounds except for the howls from two stray cats fighting somewhere. Working fast, you **climb into** the dumpster to rummage through the trash. You **keep your eyes peeled** for the half-empty, tied-up plastic bag.

After about thirty minutes of digging, you find it. Through the plastic, you see the name "Oz." You **tear it open** and look through the items inside. The name typed on the front of one particular envelope **grabs your attention**.

Frederick Foster

The name sets your **heart racing**. You think you now have proof that Franklin Oz is Frederick Foster. You start to open the envelope in your hand but stop. You hear something. Nearby, footsteps are coming your way.

Quickly, you put the envelope in your jacket pocket, **jump out of** the dumpster, and run to the front of the building. Once on the main street, you walk to the bus stop to go back to Nick's apartment. But something bothers you. You try to listen for anyone approaching you, but all you can hear is the wind.

Overhead, heavy rain clouds rumble. You can feel it in the air. A **storm is coming**.

If you are thinking about the wind and rain, go to page 101.

If you think that something bad is about to happen, go to page 106.

You are thinking about the wind and rain. You **brace yourself against** the chilly gusts. Above you, the clouds look heavy.

As the bus approaches, you open your wallet to count the **exact change** for the bus fare. You are **taken by surprise** when someone pushes you hard from behind.

"Hey!" you yell. You swing around, expecting to see Mani coming at you. But it is only a man **waving** what looks like a paper bag at you. He mumbles something you can't understand, and then staggers away down the sidewalk, drunk.

Your fear and anger **turn into** relief. Anyway, Mani already went home to his family. He couldn't be an undercover agent and a family man, could he?

Back home at Nick's apartment, you reach protectively for the envelope you **tucked away** in your jacket pocket. Frederick Foster's name was on the outside of the envelope. Maybe you will finally have the information to **piece together this puzzle**.

Nothing.

All you can feel with your hand is the smooth lining of your jacket. You **take off** the jacket and shake it. You check all the pockets again. Frantic, you try the back pocket of your jeans and inside your shirt.

The envelope isn't there. Did you drop it somewhere on the street or on the bus? Was someone really following you when you thought the **coast was clear**? You shake your head. Even if it were possible, wouldn't you have felt someone reach into your pockets? The only thing that was **out of the ordinary** was the drunk man who **ran into** you.

*He shoved me from behind—**classic move** from a pickpocket.*

You groan. The envelope is gone. You lost it. How could you have been so careless? And it might be worse than you think. The envelope and whatever was inside could now be in the **wrong hands**.

You decide to send Betty a quick message. You attach the pictures you took of the things in Oz's office. And, of course, you tell her about the missing envelope that suggests that Franklin. Oz is Frederick Foster. Betty is grateful for all you have found, but she is also apologetic you had such a **close call**. She is also concerned you lost a very important piece of evidence.

After chatting with Betty, you **lie down** on the couch. You close your eyes and try to relax, but your mind won't stop reviewing all of the day's events. There were too many **close calls** out there. Too many. And who is to blame? Was it such a good idea to go undercover with other cleaning people around? It seems that Betty didn't **think it through** very carefully.

Now you aren't so sure how much you can always depend on Betty and Cleaning House. You might have to **rely on your own instincts** more than you thought.

Go to **page 103**.

When you **wake up** the next morning, you see that Nick is eating breakfast alone. Cat isn't around.

I wonder why Cat didn't spend the night as usual.

"Morning, Nick," you say, trying to get your cousin's attention. He nods without looking up from his bowl of cereal. He just stares blankly ahead, **shoveling food** into his mouth.

Trouble in paradise?

You decide to **strike up a conversation**. "How was work?"

"Long," he answers with a sigh. "The usual."

"Did you get home before or after me?"

"Before," he answers.

"Was Cat with you?"

"Actually, no," he says, a little surprised. "She said she had to take something and **bring it over** to her boss." He looks up as you join him in the kitchen. "Where were you? Why were you out so late?"

"Oh, I just decided to go out," you answer **vaguely**.

*Cat wasn't with Nick? **Running errands** for her boss? What if—*

"**It figures**," he says with a huff, **breaking your train of thought**. "Wait until you have a *real* job like me."

"I'm going to the police station again for more interviewing," you say. "I think they have some **strong leads** on my mother."

Nick nods but doesn't ask any other questions. "I'll be working overtime again as usual."

You frown. Once again, your cousin seems preoccupied with his own **personal matters**. When is he going to **take an interest** in your mother's case?

After Nick leaves for work, you hear the familiar sound of your phone vibrating on the coffee table next to you. Betty has sent you a new message.

We need more information on Foster's daughter. Go downtown to find an old friend of the Fosters, a **masseuse** named Cynthia.

Although you are still disappointed after last night's events, you try to **stay positive** and optimistic. For not being an experienced detective, you have been able to gather a lot of clues already. You **screwed up**—losing the envelope for one—but you have also learned from your mistakes. You hope that Betty hasn't **lost faith in you**.

You try to focus on your next mission. You Google all of the salons and spas in downtown Washington, D.C. and **narrow down** the list to six spots.

Go to **page 105.**

The main streets of downtown are **hopping**, full of crowds of people, mostly tourists who are shopping or on **sightseeing tours**. There are tall **skyscrapers** and historic buildings and **landmarks** that **line** the street. Street vendors sell souvenirs on the sidewalk, and street performers entertain tourists for money. You jostle and push your way through the crowds of slow-moving people.

"Whoops! Excuse me, pardon me," you say repeatedly, though no one around you seems to be moving **out of the way**. You **bump into people** left and right.

You look at your phone screen. Your GPS shows that you are walking on a block where there are two salons that have employees named Cynthia.

"Hey you! Jerk! Why don't you **watch where you're going**?" someone yells from behind you.

You **look up** from your phone and turn to see an old man bending down over several containers of food that have spilled on the ground. You watch as people walk by, ignoring him. You keep walking too. When you look back, you see the man scrambling to **pick up** the pieces of fallen food with his shaky hands. Then he looks in your direction and yells, "Come back here! You think you can **get away** with that?"

If you think that the old man is accusing you of knocking over his food and avoiding taking responsibility, go to **page 112**.

If you think that the old man is yelling at someone else for stealing something that belongs to him, go to **page 113**.

Something bad is about to happen. Someone is following you, and you know you aren't safe.

You start running as fast as you can toward the main street where there might be traffic and people. Unfortunately, the street is empty at this hour. Rain pelts the sidewalk so hard and fast that it sounds like radio static. Even if someone were following you, there would be no way you could hear him or her through the downpour.

You **slow down** to **catch your breath**.

Breathe, just breathe.

As you approach an intersection, you **make a sharp right turn** and find yourself on a grassy patch. Right away, it is as if someone **turned down** the volume. Falling on soft earth rather than on hard pavement, the rain is less deafening here.

That is when you hear it, a pair of sneakers squeaking on the wet sidewalk several feet behind you.

Go to **page 107**.

Now you are sure that you are being followed. Luckily, you have watched enough movies and read enough crime novels to know what to do if you are being **tailed**.

> RULE 1 - Vary your speed and direction; watch to see
> if the person following you does the same thing.

Carefully, without making it obvious, you **speed up** and **turn a few more corners**. You glance at a storefront window. In the reflection, you think you see a dark figure wearing a hooded raincoat. You walk a little faster, hoping to gain a little more distance between you and that person.

Up ahead, you see a type of street that Washington, D.C. is famous for: a **traffic circle**. And it isn't just any traffic circle. It is busy Dupont Circle. You walk straight toward the large marble fountain, relieved it is still crowded with throngs of people, although they are walking faster now or huddling under umbrellas to **beat the rain**. You think you are safe . . . for now. You know you aren't **in the clear** just yet.

> RULE 2 - **Get lost** in a crowd.

You find a street that looks like it is **lined with** bars and restaurants. You hurry in that direction and stop at the first bar you see. An engraved wooden sign above the door greets you.

The Black Cat

It is crowded inside the bar. You push your way through the crowd to the back of the room where you stand against the wall, watching the door for the person in the dark raincoat.

What color was the coat? Unfortunately, it was too dark to see. *Was it black, dark blue, gray?*

You examine each person in the room, looking for someone who seems nervous or **makes eye contact**. Instead, everyone seems to be just having a good time—drinking, laughing, and talking in groups. You feel yourself relax a little.

Then you see the door open. A person in a dark, hooded raincoat steps inside. The person **takes off** his hood, revealing an athletic man with a mustache, beard, and a scar through his right eyebrow. You don't recognize him at all. He **narrows his eyes** and **scans** the room with a scowl. He **makes eye contact** with you, and then looks away. To your horror, he slowly reaches into his coat.

For a **split second**, you imagine him **pulling out** a gun.

*Bullets fly through the air and **tear** into the crowded bar. You hear the screams of people around you. Backed against the far wall, you are trapped. All you can do is watch in horror as people fall to the ground in **pools of blood**.*

You blink.

The man pulls out . . . a phone.

He starts texting. Then he **looks up** and nods in your direction. You are **frozen** in place. He is coming your way. You **stand up** to confront him. Before you can say anything, the man walks right past you and up to a nervous young woman with curly hair sitting at the bar. They hug awkwardly as he apologizes.

"Autumn, right? I'm Josh," the man says. "So sorry I'm late. I couldn't get a cab because of the rain, so I had to walk. Nice to meet you . . . officially."

You feel foolish. Your cousin is right. Maybe you have been letting your crime stories affect your thinking. *I'm turning into a mental case* . . . You shake your head, confused. But your instincts can't be wrong. Someone *was* following you outside. You are sure of it. Whoever it was, you heard his or her sneakers squeak on the wet sidewalk after you **made a sharp turn**.

"Do you want something?"

You jump. A petite bartender with bright red hair waits for your order. Her nametag says "Stephanie." You recognize the name but **can't put your finger on it**.

"Um . . . " you start to say.

"You okay? You're pale and **sweating all over the place**."

"No, I'm fine," you try to say normally. "It's the rain."

She raises an eyebrow, unconvinced.

"Just give me the cheapest beer you have **on tap**."

"Be right back," she answers. "Just don't **die on me**."

After a few minutes, the bartender returns with your beer and puts the glass on a napkin. You tell her to **keep the change**, and she nods gratefully.

As you drink your beer, you realize how angry you are—angry that you are **second-guessing** yourself again. You take a **long sip** of your drink. Your **head is spinning** now. Hungry and tipsy, you feel more foolish than ever.

Was someone following me . . . or was it just my insecurities ***sneaking up on*** *me?*

If you think that there was definitely someone following you, go to **page 110**.

If you think that there was no one following you, and that it was just your nerves, go to **page 111**.

There was definitely someone following you. And not just anyone but someone who has been very interested in you since the day you arrived in D.C.—a person who always wears sneakers.

Cat, how very sneaky of you . . .

Now the question remains: Who does Cat work for? Who is her **handler**? You can think of two names: Betty or Foster. Betty might have hired Cat to **shadow you**—but for what reason? Or maybe Foster might be the one **calling the shots** with Cat—in which case, Cat would definitely be dangerous.

Then you have a disturbing thought. You reach into your jacket pocket for the envelope addressed to Foster but **come up empty**. The envelope is gone.

"Shit," you say out loud.

You pound the counter with your fists. You know you got **ahead of yourself**. You **have no business** trying to handle this case on your own. You are just an amateur who reads too many books. You order another beer and ponder your **sorry situation**. From now on, you decide you need to rely on Betty. She is the real expert here, not you.

Exhausted and humbled, you **chug** the rest of your beer, **pay your tab**, and decide to take a cab home. No more heroics. You will get a **good night's sleep**, you decide, and wait patiently for Betty's next orders.

Go to **page 103**.

No one following you, and it was just your nerves. You are being paranoid. You laugh at yourself and **chug** the rest of your beer. It was only your **imagination getting the best of you**.

The bartender was right. Time to relax.

Already, you can feel the beer **doing a number** on your head. You take the napkin to wipe the sweat off your forehead and notice some writing on it.

NICE TRY

You twist around in your seat to find the bartender, Stephanie, but she is nowhere in sight.

Oh no. Did she . . .

You reach inside your jacket pocket to check, and sure enough the envelope addressed to Foster is gone.

"Shit," you mumble.

Feeling sick now and **woozy** from the beer, you decide that it is best to **hail a cab** and go home to **lick your wounds**.

Go to **page 134**.

The old man is accusing you of knocking over his food and avoiding **taking responsibility**. You walk back and apologize. "I didn't know I **ran into you**," you say, kneeling down next to him. "If I knew it was me, I'd have stopped to help."

"Maybe if you weren't so busy looking down at your phone," the old man says, scolding you as you help him up. "All young people do these days is look at their phones. You're all clueless. If you don't start **paying attention**, you'll get to my age and realize that **life has passed you by**."

You start to feel guilty. He is right. By not being observant, you are going to miss important clues.

"Anyway, we can't just leave this mess out here on the sidewalk," the old man continues. He points to a store. "Why don't you go there and ask for something to clean this up?"

At the store, you borrow a broom and dustpan from the owners. When you return, the old man pulls the broom out of your hands and starts sweeping: three short sweeps, followed by three long sweeps.

"We've **got your back**, young man," he says plainly and then walks away.

When you return the broom and dustpan to the store, you see it. Above an entrance next to the store is a big, bright sign that makes you smile.

Serenity Spa

Go to **page 114**.

The old man is yelling at someone else for stealing something that belongs to him. But you don't notice anyone suspicious running through the crowd. Why would anyone try to rob an old man anyway?

You continue walking down the street with your GPS, looking for the next salon on your list. Will someone give you a signal? There is no one standing around sweeping, just crowds of people walking on the sidewalk. What if you go inside and make an appointment with the wrong Cynthia? You could spend hours getting a massage for no reason. You know you can't **afford to waste any time**.

"Get your free local paper! It's the *DC Express!*" A man standing in the middle of the sidewalk pushes a folded newspaper right into your hands.

You are about to toss the paper in the trash when you notice the front-page headline: "Local Woman **Gets Away** with Murder." Curious, you continue to read the first three lines of the article. It is about a woman who robs a store and kills a store employee. The police arrive before she can escape, but thinking she is just a witness, they release her after only a few questions.

*The woman **got away** with it.*

The old man and his words come to mind. He was yelling at you because *you* made him drop his food. He was saying that you were trying to **get away with it**, trying to leave without **facing the consequences**.

Go to **page 112**.

The spa is located on the third floor. At the front desk you ask the receptionist for the next available appointment with Cynthia. "You're **in luck**. There's been a cancellation," the receptionist tells you, checking her computer screen. "Cynthia can take you in twenty minutes. **Have a seat**."

You wait in the spa's quiet sitting room. The scents of lavender and lemon fill the air. Despite your nervousness, you can't help but relax a little.

Soon, a woman with long black hair comes out and calls your name. You follow her to a dim private room where she tells you to undress and get under a sheet on the table. "I'll return in a few minutes," she says.

Nervous, you get undressed and get on the massage table. You lie on your stomach and place your face on the cushioned hole on the massage table. Then you reach behind you and pull the sheet over your legs and lower back.

"Are you ready?" Cynthia asks, knocking on the door.

"Come in."

Cynthia walks in like she is **floating on air** and turns on some soft, calming music. The room fills with the sounds of flutes and wind chimes. You can hear her putting oil in her hands and rubbing them together.

"Is this your first time getting a massage?" she asks.

You are so **tongue-tied** that all you can do is nod. You feel Cynthia start to massage the back of your head and neck, working away the **knots** in your muscles. You feel yourself start to relax and **melt** into the table. If you don't stay focused and alert, you might just fall asleep. Time for an **icebreaker**.

"Where are you from?" you try to ask as naturally as you can.

"Houston, Texas."

"Oh, really?" you say with surprise. "What a **coincidence**."

She stops massaging your neck for a moment. "You're also from Houston?" Her voice sounds friendlier.

You nod your head.

"Which neighborhood did you **grow up** in?"

You pause. You realize you should have done more research on Foster's case. What can you say now?

"Uh, you know what? I was so young when I lived there. I can't remember the name of it ... I think it sounded like—"

"Let me guess," Cynthia interrupts, moving down to massage your shoulders. "Was it River Oaks?"

You pause to create suspense. "You're good."

She slaps your back with some force. "I can't believe it," she laughs. "**What are the chances**?"

"My family was good friends with the Fosters."

"You're kidding!" she says. "Our families were good friends too. Then, you must have been friends with Frida."

Frida must be Frederick's daughter. You try to **contain your excitement**.

"Well, my family moved out of the neighborhood when I turned five. I only knew Frida briefly. She was a nice girl from **the little I can remember**." You want to keep Cynthia talking. "What do you remember about her?"

"Oh, she had a real talent for theater back then. She wanted to be an actress or a singer **from day one**. I'll never forget when she played the character Dorothy in the *Wizard of Oz* in fifth grade. Her dad was so proud of her."

So Frida could be the little girl in the photo! You feel your **heart beat faster** and try not to show the excitement in your voice. "Are you still in contact with her? Do you have any idea where she is now?"

"No," she says sadly. "I haven't talked to her in years. Not since ... well, you know, she disappeared with her mother after her father **got busted**. I tried to find her on Facebook a few years ago, but I think maybe her mother changed her name."

"Got busted? Did something happen to the family?" you say, pretending to be shocked.

Cynthia stops massaging you. You feel a cold spot on your back from where she has removed her hands.

"Don't tell me you don't know what happened."

You pretend to be completely unaware. "Sorry."

"Frederick was arrested for work he did for some **drug ring**. I don't know if I believe it because he was such a nice person. I used to go to their house a lot and never noticed **anything out of the ordinary**. Anyway, his wife **ran away** with Frida. I guess she couldn't handle the controversy. It's all so **heartbreaking**. Frida always **looked up to** her father. He was her hero, and he adored her more than anything. Now it seems like he's **lost all contact** with her."

"Wow, I can't believe all that happened to them. They were such nice people. But don't you think there had to be good evidence for Mr. Foster to be **put away**?"

At the mention of evidence, Cynthia gets quiet. Her hands have returned to your back, but her strokes are more intense. It feels as if she is kneading dough. Finally, she says, "So you were neighbors with them until you were five, right? What's your name again?"

"David."

"David what?" she asks, asking for your full name.

At first, you don't want to answer her. You try to control your breathing and stay calm. You shift uncomfortably on the table as the strokes on your back get harder and harder.

"Am I **rubbing you the wrong way**?"

If you think that Cynthia is asking you whether her massage technique hurts, go to **page 117**.

If you think that Cynthia is asking you whether something she said bothers you, go to **page 124**.

Cynthia is asking you whether her massage technique hurts. "No, you're not **rubbing me the wrong way**," you answer through gritted teeth. "This is the best massage I've ever had." You try to **cover up** your nervous voice with a laugh, "Well, actually, it's the only massage I've ever had."

In one swift motion, Cynthia pulls something down over the massage table. Wide leather straps cut into your back and arms. You can't move.

"Well, something about you **rubs me the wrong way**," she snaps.

"Hey! What are you doing?"

"Don't give me that 'I'm innocent' **routine**. Who are you?" She pulls the straps tighter, pinning your body on the table. "I think you're trying to get information from me," Cynthia says angrily. She pulls out her cell phone. "Frederick Foster is my friend, and I don't **rat on** my friends for any reason. Understand? If you're trying to collect evidence or use my **testimony** against him, I don't want **anything to do with it**."

She then walks out of the room and slams the door, leaving you strapped to the table and unable to move. Lifting your head, you see that the straps are pulled tight over your body. There is no way you can wriggle your whole torso free. You try moving your arms. The massage oil on your shoulders makes it easier to twist around. You manage to slide down far enough to free an elbow, and then the other. Clasping your hands together on your back, you push the emergency button on your watch.

Hurry, you pray. Who knows what Cynthia will do to you when she gets back.

Ten minutes later, Betty bursts through the door. You have never felt so much relief. Without saying anything, she uses a pocketknife to slash at the straps and **cut you loose**. After you **throw on** your clothes, Betty motions for you to follow her down a set of stairs in the back of the spa.

"Are you sure this is the right way?" you ask.

Betty looks at you. "This is no time to be **dragging your feet!**"

If you think that Betty is worried that you can't run fast enough, go to **page 119.**

If you think that Betty is worried that you are losing your confidence in her and having doubts, go to **page 122.**

Betty is worried that you can't run fast enough and that you won't be able to escape before Cynthia gets back. But you aren't **dragging your feet**—you are trying to run as fast as you can. Cynthia's threats have really **left an impression on you**; you are just scared. What if Betty hadn't arrived there **in time**? What would Foster have done to you while you were strapped to the table, naked and unable to move?

"I'm trying to hurry," you insist, though you are struggling to **keep up with** Betty. Your lungs burn from the effort. You wonder how she can run so fast, how she seems to know exactly where she is going in an unfamiliar building. Racing down the stairs and turning through the tunnels of hallways in the basement, Betty doesn't **miss a beat**.

Once outside, you see a car—your **getaway**, a fast-looking Porsche. You stare at the sleek sports car **in awe**. You have never seen one **in person**.

"This is our ride. Get in," Betty instructs.

She disappears into the driver's side, but not before **flashing you** an amused smile. The engines **roar to life**, and within seconds you are halfway down the street. Through the tinted windows, you watch the buildings move past you in a blur. Only when you are several blocks away does Betty start to talk.

"I'm sorry we **put you in danger** like that," Betty says quietly, her eyes **glued to the road**. "Our sources didn't know that Cynthia was still in close contact with Foster. We were informed she was close to the daughter, not the father. We didn't think she'd react that way. I hope you're not losing confidence."

"If I hadn't made her suspicious, she might have given me Frederick's contact information. I'm sorry. I **dropped the ball on this one**."

"No, you don't understand. I meant losing confidence in *me*. I saw you hesitate back there. I know you have your doubts. But I still think we're **on the right track**. If my instincts are correct, Cynthia can still lead us to him. You **spooked** her. I'm sure she's alerted Frederick by now and told him that Cleaning House is **on his trail**." She pauses to shift gears. "He might even know that Ana's son is looking for her now."

You don't like the sound of that. "I don't think I'm very good at this," you say. "I get too nervous. I say too much—"

"You can't **give up**, David," Betty reassures you.

"What if you hadn't showed up?"

"We've been tracking you this whole time. We got to you **in time**, didn't we?"

Betty is right. She came to get you only ten minutes after you pushed the button on your watch. Still, you have your doubts. You aren't so sure Betty or anyone else from Cleaning House can be there all the time. What if the next time you need help she comes too late?

"I'm not **cut out for this**," you say.

Betty **pulls over** the car to the side of the road and looks you directly in the eyes. "All you can do is try your best. David, this is serious now. From my experience, when someone is kidnapped or goes missing for more than a week, it's much more likely that they **end up** dead."

Betty's words are like a slap to the face. You are horrified at the thought of never finding your mother.

Betty continues, in a gentler voice. "We can still find Ana, but we're **running out of time**. Our chances are good. You found proof that Franklin Oz *is* Frederick Foster. Now his **cover is blown**. You got information about his daughter, Frida. To be honest, we'd probably hire you . . . if you had more confidence."

You nod without a word.

"**Listen up**. This is what I want you to do next. Our sources tell us that Foster has been **spotted** around town. A barista working at the Starbucks on the campus of American University might know something. He's one of our **informants**. We believe this is a **good**

lead because American University is one of your mother's 'cleaning sites.' In fact, it's the last place your mother visits on her shift. Find that barista and make sure you give our informant **a good tip** for the tip you get."

Go to **page 127**.

Betty is worried that you are losing your confidence in her and having doubts, that you are **dragging your feet** because you are unsure she knows what she is doing. The **truth of the matter** is she is right. You aren't sure if you truly trust her abilities. You aren't sure of a lot of things anymore.

You have so many questions swirling around your head. How did Cleaning House let Foster out of their sight? None of this would have happened if they had taken your mother's warnings more seriously. And if Cleaning House can't protect its own detectives from harm, how can they protect you? You start to wonder if you are **better off** trying to find your mother **on your own**.

Once outside, Betty leads you to a car—and not just any car. You stare at a sleek Porsche **in awe**. You blink. You have never seen one **in person**. "That's yours?" you stammer.

"This is our **getaway**," Betty says.

You see her disappear into the driver's side but not before **flashing you** a smile. The engine **roars to life**. Within seconds, you are halfway down the street. Through the tinted windows, you watch the buildings **fly past you** in a blur. Only when you are several blocks away from the salon does Betty start to talk.

"I'm sorry I **put you in danger** like that," she says. "I promise it won't happen again."

"Really?" you say angrily. "Because that was a **close call**." You cringe when you remember the tight leather straps holding you down. It was terrifying.

"Part of the job, David."

You shake your head, not trying to hide your disbelief.

"Anyway, I'm confident we're **closing in** on Foster," Betty adds. "In fact, I have a **good lead** on where he was seen last. I'll send you a message about it soon."

Another mission? Is she really serious? You start to think it might be best if you start **making your own plans**, separate from Betty's, **just in case**.

"Sure," you reply, staring straight ahead.

There is nothing else to do but **head back** to Nick's apartment. You stay quiet as Betty shifts gears smoothly and **weaves through traffic**.

Go to **page 134**.

Cynthia is asking you whether something she said bothers you. "No, you're not **rubbing me the wrong way**. I'm just so surprised to hear about what happened to Frederick."

"And I'm surprised that you didn't know about it," she says suspiciously. "Since your families were such good friends."

"Well, we haven't been **in touch** with the Fosters for a long time."

She looks at you for a moment. "Tell me your last name again."

"Uh, Lopez," you lie.

"Strange. That doesn't **ring a bell**."

You can tell you are losing her trust. Then you have an idea. If Cynthia grew up with the Fosters, she probably also knew your mother. And if Cynthia knew the truth that Frederick was out of prison, and that Frida and your mother were in trouble, wouldn't she want to help?

You sit up on the table. "That's because I'm lying," you answer with a sigh. You know it is risky to reveal yourself, but, at this moment, you aren't sure what else to do.

Cynthia **backs away** from you. "What? Who are you?"

"My name is David. My mother, Ana, was the Fosters' housekeeper years ago. She's the one who **found out** Frederick Foster was involved in the **drug ring**. After he went to prison, my mother was relocated here to D.C. Soon after Foster got out of prison, my mother **went missing**. I think he might have kidnapped her and is looking for Frida so he can take back his fortune."

Cynthia's face **turns white**. "You're Ana's son?"

You nod. "I'm working undercover to find out as much as I can about the Fosters. Then maybe I can find my mother."

"**Serves him right** then," Cynthia says quietly, sitting next to you on the massage table. "I knew your mother. She was the nicest lady. Frida loved her. So did I. She treated us like her daughters. If Foster is responsible . . . " Her voice **trails off**.

You feel a **lump form in your throat**. "Yes, my mother is a good person. And a good mother. I have to find her. Can you help?"

Cynthia squeezes your shoulder to reassure you. "I'll do whatever I can."

"Can you try to **look up** Frida for me? If you hear from her or have any more information, please let me know."

After you add her on Facebook, you thank Cynthia for her help, pay her for the massage, and say goodbye. It feels good to tell the truth again. For the first time in a long time, you believe in yourself.

As you are leaving the salon, you feel your phone vibrate in your pocket with a new message from Cynthia.

> I wasn't completely honest with you. I've been **in touch** with Frida recently. I was just trying to protect her, but I can see you are sincere. She was living in New York, but I heard she's back in town to **star in** some show at the National Theater. She's going by the name of 'Dorothy.' I'm sorry for **keeping you in the dark**.

Here is another **solid lead** on Foster. You see how it is all **coming together** now: the "Franklin Oz" alias, the photo of the little girl in the costume, the *Yellow Brick Road* CD. These are all connected to *The Wizard of Oz*. Frida is going by the name 'Dorothy,' the main character in that film.

You go to a local library and spend hours searching through videos clips from the film. One scene **catches your attention**. Throughout her journey, Dorothy looks for a way to return home. When she reaches the Emerald City, even the Wizard of Oz can't help her. With the help of the Good Witch though, Dorothy realizes that she has the ability to get home on her own. Dorothy shuts her eyes and clicks the heels of her red shoes together, while repeating the now-famous line: "There's **no place like home**."

You replay the video clip again and again. "There's no place like home," echoes the famous line.

Where have I heard that line before?

You shake your head and try to focus. You have to find Frida. Whatever her part was in your mother's kidnapping, she is the one direct link to Foster.

You send Betty a message, telling her about the evidence you have gathered and your latest thoughts on the investigation. Betty replies quickly.

> We've been **covering a lot of ground**. I'll send you our next **lead** tomorrow. Go home and get some rest.

Go to **page 134.**

The Starbucks near the American University campus is crowded with customers. You watch carefully for one of the baristas to give you the signal, but they all seem busy taking orders and making coffee. None of them are cleaning or sweeping.

You get in line. At the counter, a female barista looks at you and smiles. "How can I help you, sir?"

"I'm David," you say slowly. *Okay, give me a signal . . .*

"Hi, David," she answers. "How can I **take your order**?"

You stand there, waiting for her to do something. The barista sighs and waits for your answer. Finally, you answer, "I'd like a vanilla cappuccino. A grande."

The barista **punches your order** on the register and tells you the total. You **stall for time**, looking for money in your wallet. You want to give her another chance to give you a signal, but the barista just stands there and waits. After you pay her, you stand in another line to wait for another barista to make your coffee and call your name. Did you come to the right coffee shop? Was Betty's source correct?

"David," a person calls out, interrupting your thoughts. You watch the man put a large cup of coffee on the counter.

Then you have an idea. As you grab your coffee, you purposefully spill a container of sugar on the floor.

"My fault. Sorry for the mess," you say out loud.

"I'm **on it**," says a tall, male barista sporting thick, black-framed glasses and tattoos. He grabs a broom and starts to **sweep away** the white grains. You watch as he moves the broom: three short sweeps and three long sweeps. You follow him to the corner of the room.

"The guy you're looking for came in here earlier this morning," the barista whispers to you. "He was arguing with someone on his cell phone—told the person he had to go somewhere this evening. He said 'she' might be there at the National . . . something. The National Mall, maybe? I'm not sure." The barista sniffs. "He wasn't a very nice customer either—didn't even tip me."

You make sure you don't make the same mistake and **slip him** a crisp five-dollar bill, putting the money into the male barista's hands. A tip for a tip, like Betty said.

If you think that the National Mall is a national park in the city with museums, monuments, and other landmarks and important sites, go to **page 129**.

If you think that the National Mall is a big shopping center in the city, go to **page 130**.

The National Mall is a national park in the city with museums, monuments, and other landmarks and important sites. Why would Frederick risk going to such a public place?

You find a taxi and tell the driver to take you to The National Mall. About ten minutes later, the taxi driver **pulls over** and parks on Constitution Avenue. "We're here," he says.

You look out the window. All you see are hills, fields of grass, and a gigantic statue that looks like a **pillar** with a point at the top. You remember seeing this pillar in souvenir shops. Then you realize it is **The Washington Monument**, one of the most famous monuments in Washington, D.C. You wish you could enjoy it for a moment, but you know you don't have time.

"This is The National Mall? Where do I go now?"

"Where do you want to go?" he says, shrugging. "The National Mall is a big place. It's basically a park. You should get yourself a tour guide or a map."

"I'm not sure what I'm looking for."

"Well, you can start there." He points in the direction of an open area filled with people. "There's an international festival happening this weekend. See those white tents between the Capitol Building and the Washington Monument? I'd start there. **Grab a bite to eat**. Check out the cultural stuff. Good luck, though, because it's going to be crowded."

You pay the fare and thank the taxi driver, and then dash toward the festival area.

Go to **page 131**.

The National Mall is a big shopping center in the city. Not wanting to waste any time, you jump in the first taxi you see and tell the driver to take you to the mall. At first, the driver seems confused and doesn't know where to take you.

"Isn't there a big shopping mall in D.C.? I have to meet someone at the mall. Please hurry."

When you get to the Georgetown shopping center, you are confused. You wish you had gotten more information from the barista. You look at your phone, but there are no new messages from Betty. *This is a **dead end**,* you think as you stare at the crowded stores around you filled with people.

One of the stores **grabs your attention**, and you wander toward it. The sign above the entrance says "D.C. Souvenir Central." On the shelves are books, posters, and clothing with images of the city, as well as miniature statues that are replicas of the national monuments. On the wall, you notice a calendar for sale. The front of the calendar says "Scenes from The National Mall." Each month has a picture of a different national monument or site: the Lincoln Memorial, the Washington Memorial, the World War II Memorial, the Jefferson Memorial, the Martin Luther King, Jr. Memorial, the Capitol building, the White House, and so on.

It finally **dawns on you**: The National Mall isn't a shopping mall at all.

Go to **page 129**.

Thousands of tourists fill the festival area, eating, drinking, listening to folk singers and rock bands, and watching performers dance in colorful costumes. Each tent area offers **a taste** of a different national culture from around the world. Sadly, everyone but you seems to be laughing and having a good time. You are desperate and frustrated by your lack of progress. You feel like a rock in a stream, people moving around you like currents of water. Are there any Cleaning House agents here?

Catching you off guard, someone grabs your arm and pulls you into one of the white tents. You are surprised to see a tiny elderly woman wearing large hoop earrings and colorful scarves wrapped around her hair. "Come, young man," she says, **flashing you** a smile and her one gold tooth. "I've been waiting for you."

"Sorry, lady," you say, trying to pull away from her surprisingly strong grip. "I don't have time for this right now."

But the woman doesn't listen to you and nudges you over to a round table with a **crystal ball** in the middle. She is a **fortune-teller**. You have seen many women like her back home. Most of the time, they prowl the city streets, looking for tourists to fool, charging money for so-called "visions of the future."

She asks you to wait while she **dusts off** the chair. You notice her hands: three short wipes and three longer wipes. It is a **long shot** but maybe she is from Cleaning House.

"I am Miss Jesica," the woman declares in a deep, husky voice. "And I have a message for you."

Nervous again, you look back at the entrance of the tent warily. If you need to escape, you can **slip away** with ease. The woman **snaps her fingers** to **grab your attention**.

"I see it now. You are lost, young man. You have **lost yourself!**" She stares into her crystal ball, her eyes intense with feeling.

You nod, **keeping your eyes on** the people passing by the tent. You try to pretend you are bored, but you are **shaken** by her words and the expression on her face.

Well, it's true though, you think. *I've lost my mother and now I feel lost myself.*

"You have **lost touch** with yourself over the past few years. You don't know who you are." The woman's voice rises. "But I have good news! If you can **get in touch** with yourself and your family again, things will become **crystal clear**."

"I hope you don't think I'm paying you for this," you protest, though you are amazed at her words, which are oddly accurate.

"Go now," continues the woman, pointing her bony finger at the entrance of the tent. "Just remember: There's **no place like home**."

Walking out of the tent, you feel dazed and confused. You try to **brush off** what the woman said as nonsense, but you **can't help but** think about her words. *Get in touch with myself? No place like home? Does it all mean something important?*

Desperately, you look at your phone, but there are still no new messages from Betty.

If you decide to wait for someone to contact you, go to **page 133**.

If the **fortune-teller**'s advice encourages you to think about your life, go to **page 175**.

You decide to wait for someone to contact you. If the **fortune-teller** is working for Cleaning House, then she must be telling you that Betty will help.

With some reluctance, you decide to wait patiently for Betty to **get in touch** with you and **make the call** on what to do next. You **spend the rest of the day** at the festival before going home later that evening.

Go to **page 134**.

When you arrive back at Nick's apartment, all is quiet. The living room is empty and the bedroom door is closed. You try not to make too much noise as you make your way inside. You walk slowly on the wood floors, trying not to make them creak. In the dark, your footsteps seem louder than usual. Then a noise **breaks your concentration**.

Tap.

The sound is coming from the front door. You wait and listen in the dark.

Tap, tap.

Cautiously, you reach for the doorknob and open the door. No one is there. You walk outside. The walkway in front of the apartment building looks empty. All you can hear is the rustling of the wind.

Then a bright flash by the mailboxes **catches your attention**. It looks like a light. You realize it is the reflection of the street lamp on something—something you recognize all too well: a piece of jewelry, a bright blue jewel on an antique silver ring.

Cat steps **out of the shadows** and stands squarely in front of you. From **head to toe**, she is dressed entirely in black, except for a pair of familiar-looking sneakers. Draped on her arm is a black hooded raincoat.

"It's time to **give up**," she declares.

If you think that Cat is saying that she will finally reveal her true identity, go to **page 135**.

If you think that Cat is saying that you should stop trying to be detective, go to **page 143**.

Cat is saying that she will finally reveal her true identity. Maybe Cat has decided to stop pretending to be Nick's girlfriend and **give up her act**.

"Well, it's about time—" you start to say.

"Shh," Cat whispers, pointing up toward the apartment window. "Nick doesn't need to know about this. He's a good person. I don't want him to get involved. He thinks I'm his girlfriend, so that's what I'll be."

"You're going to keep lying to him? How long are you going to **keep this up**?"

Cat ignores your question. "It's time to **give *him* up**."

You are confused. So Cat wasn't talking about Nick.

"Who?" you ask.

Do you finally trust Cat to give you a **straight answer**?

If you trust Cat to tell you the truth, go to page 137.

If you don't trust Cat to tell you the truth, go to page 140.

[CHAPTER FOUR]

~ Looking for This?

YOU TRUST CAT to tell you the truth. While you have always doubted her, especially after all the strange interactions you have had together, in this moment she looks desperate. Her eyes are watering with tears, and she is trembling with heavy sighs. She looks ready to give you a **straight answer**.

"Let's go inside," you say, leading her gently by the arm.

At the kitchen table inside the apartment, she bursts into tears. "Fred . . . that bastard," she sobs.

"Fred—Frederick Foster?"

Hearing Cat say the name of your number one suspect fills you with **dread**. You hand her a tissue, and she blows her nose.

"I've been spying on your cousin and your mother for six months now . . . for him," Cat confesses. "If it wasn't for me, he wouldn't have found your mother and kidnapped her." She looks at you apologetically. "That was **business, nothing personal**."

"Go on."

"So, I was just Fred's employee—until I wasn't."

"Oh," you say with understanding. Cat became romantically involved with Foster.

"He promised me that after I helped him find his daughter and kill your mother, we'd take all of his money and move someplace far away—Thailand. But it looks like he's made the same promise to another one of his partners . . . "

Then she pulls out a familiar envelope from her purse. "Looking for this?"

It is the envelope addressed to Foster that you lost earlier. "But how did you . . . ?" you start to say. You begin to realize that Betty was right. *No one is who you think they are.* "It was you. You stole it."

She tosses the envelope to you. You reach inside and pull out a letter and start reading it out loud.

"**It goes without saying** that I love you—"

"Ugh, stop," Cat yells, putting her hands over her ears. "I thought it was something else, but it's actually a letter from another agent who works for him."

"Another agent? Someone else works for Foster?"

"Her name is Stephanie. Some redhead. That asshole made her the same promise. But you know what? I don't care anymore. I don't love him. My job is to make men fall **in love** with *me*." Cat's green eyes are bright with rage. "What really **pisses me off** is that he isn't treating me as his equal. I'm a professional, you know. I'm the best damn agent he has."

You don't know what to say. You just stare at her in shock.

"But I have an idea," Cat continues, grabbing your wrists. "You and I can work together to put Fred back in prison."

"Wait," you answer angrily, yanking away your hands. "You think the two of us are going to work together now? Why should I trust you when you work for him?"

"Worked," she corrects you. "**Past is passed**. You and I both need each other now to get what we want: I want to **get back at** Fred; you want to save your mother."

"No," you say. "How can I trust you, Cat? Besides, I have other ways to save my mother."

She points at your wrist and laughs. "You really think that little spy watch can help you? Fred is too smart for Cleaning House. In Texas, he got away from them, disappeared **right under their noses**. The only person who can help you save your mother now is me. I know the guy. I can **bring him down**—"

The bedroom door swings open, and you both go silent.

"Catfish?" you hear a sleepy voice call out in the dark. "Is that you, Baby?"

Cat shakes her head at you.

"No, Nick," you lie. "It's just me. Uh, I'm just getting some water."

"Huh?"

"You're dreaming, man. Go back to bed."

"Oh, okay." You hear the door close again.

"Think about my offer," Cat continues after a few moments. "Remember, Nick knows nothing about this. And don't tell Cleaning House either. **Keep this quiet**. We'll be **in touch**."

Cat leaves the apartment as quietly as a cat prowling in the night.

Go to **page 141**.

You don't trust Cat to tell you the truth. Why should you? She has never given you a **straight answer**. It has always been **mixed signals** with her. You can't believe anything she says. She could be trying to confuse you, pretending to be **on your side**. She could be **lying through her teeth**.

Without thinking, you blurt out, "**Drop the act**, Cat. I know who you are."

"My act? I'm not talking about me. I'm talking about you. **Give up** the 'Kevin' act, David."

Go to **page 143**.

When you wake up the next morning, Nick is in the kitchen singing to himself and making breakfast for you in the kitchen. He smiles and gives you a hot plate of eggs, bacon, and toast, and a cup of coffee.

"Morning!" Nick says brightly.

"Good morning," you say back.

Your stomach is **twisted with guilt**. Nick is **clueless** that the woman he loves is an imposter. And now you, his own cousin, agreed to help her keep that secret from him. How will you continue this **charade** when you see him and Cat together?

"Hey, we can talk now since Cat didn't stay here last night," he says.

"Oh? Where is she? I thought you two were inseparable," you say, curious about the excuse she gave him.

"Something about an old friend coming to town this weekend. I guess he's staying at her apartment, and she needs to clean up."

You give him a questioning look, but he **brushes you off**. "Kiddo, don't worry. I completely trust her. But you know what? It means a lot to me that you're worried. It means you're **watching my back**." Nick slaps you hard on the shoulder.

"**Keep a watchful eye** is all I'm saying."

Nick's smile disappears, and you can see doubt forming in his eyes. He sits down at the table with you. "Anyway, what are you doing today? I have to work a **double shift** again, so you're on your own all day and tonight."

"Well, remember I told you that the police are finally getting some good **leads** on my mother?"

Nick nods, chewing his toast.

"Well, they've brought some witnesses into the station, and they want to see if I can help link any of their testimony to things I know about my mother." Your voice is steady and believable. It is the best lie you have told so far, and it disturbs you that you are getting so good at it.

"Okay, Kiddo. Is there anything else you want to talk about?"

You wish you could tell Nick everything: what you know about your mother, about your mission and the work you are doing with Cleaning House, and about Cat—especially what you know about Cat. You want desperately to **come clean**. Should you keep Nick **in the dark**?

If you think that you should tell Nick everything, go to **page 179**.

If you think that you should avoid telling Nick anything, go to **page 218**.

Cat is saying that you should stop trying to be detective. She knows you are simply an amateur, pretending **at best**. She's **on to you**. But how did she find out?

"I don't know what you're talking about," you say, slowly backing away from her.

She pulls out an envelope from her pocket. "Looking for this?"

You realize it is the envelope you lost earlier. She must have been following you or had someone else follow you to steal it.

Cat holds out her hand and gives you a dangerous look. "Does that convince you that I'm serious? Now, **give up** your watch."

You reach for your watch, feeling for the emergency button. "It's too late, Cat."

Cat simply smiles at you. Then she grabs both of your wrists, twists your arms behind you, and throws you hard, face first, against the wall. In your mouth, you taste blood. Cat pulls your watch off your wrist easily. "Got it," she exclaims. "Now she can open the safe with the code. We'll be rich."

You are confused. *Who is this 'she'?*

"Don't you work for Foster?" you ask, touching your cut lip.

"Who—Foster? No, he's actually still in prison," Cat says dismissively. She holds up the envelope. "You'd have **figured it out** if you had read the notes inside. They're letters that Foster wrote to his daughter recently. The dates **give it away**. Somehow Ana **got a hold** of them—maybe she got them from Frida, that little bitch."

You understand now. "My mother was hoping to leave them as a clue for me—to prove that Foster *wasn't* **behind this**," you say.

"**Bingo. You got it**, Detective. Luckily for me, you're an **easy mark**. It wasn't very hard to get the envelope." Cat **blows you a kiss**.

"If it isn't Foster, then who's responsible?"

She sighs impatiently. "Our wonderful mentor, of course. And by the way, thank you for pressing the button. You just let my boss know that I've got you."

You think for a moment. *Mentor?*

Suddenly, **waves of nausea hit you**. There is only one person who can claim to be helping you so far. "Betty."

All this time she was actually the one who was **pulling the strings**. How could you have missed it? You remember now how both Cat and Betty showed a strong interest in your watch. You were **blinded** by your desire to prove yourself. You admired Betty's authority and confidence, and you liked it when she showed concern for you. Dazzled by the idea of being a real agent, you **let your guard down**.

Cat flashes you a triumphant smile. "When Frederick Foster was sent to prison, his money was **up for grabs**. Corrupt cops, the Justice Department, the drug cartels—they were all after it. Ana always had a **soft spot** for Foster's daughter, Frida, so she decided she'd hide the money for her. Betty found out about it and had other ideas."

"I just can't believe it," you mumble, still in shock.

You realize now that Betty wasn't telling you the **whole story** at the Laundromat that day. It was actually Betty who wanted revenge against your mother, not Foster. She had helped Ana put Foster **behind bars**, but she didn't get any credit for it. For an ambitious agent like Betty, being overlooked in a high-profile case must have been too much.

"Betty deserves something for helping put Foster in prison all those years ago. She never got any recognition for his capture—and now she wants her **fair share**. Sad really. All Betty ever wanted was a **piece of that pie**."

"Betty doesn't want recognition—she wants to **clean out** my mother," you say, disgusted.

"You could **put it that way**. But hey—we can't all be **saints** like Ana." Cat **circles in** on you, holding something in her hand. "Now, what will we do with you?" she says, the menace growing in her voice.

You think about Nick asleep in his room. Too bad you have been keeping your cousin **in the dark**. If you yell for him now and reveal everything, would he believe you?

"Ni—!" you try to scream, but Cat covers your mouth with a wet cloth, muffling your voice. You start to cough as you breathe in the chemicals in the soaked cloth.

From the hallway, you hear the sound of footsteps coming toward you.

I have to warn him. If only I could—

Something hits the back of your head, and everything **goes dark**.

Go to **page 146**.

Still **groggy**, you can barely open your eyes or move your body when you **come to**, but you can hear Cat and Nick whispering over your head.

"Is he going to be okay?" you hear Nick ask. "I hit him too hard."

"He's just **knocked out** for a little bit. The chemicals will **wear off** soon, and he's going to be in a lot of pain when he **wakes up**. Wait here with him. I have to give the watch to Betty. Don't **let him out of your sight** until this is all over."

"I won't." You feel Nick place two fingers on your neck to check your pulse. "Are you sure he'll be fine?"

Cat lets out a snort. "Your cousin will live. I'll let you know when we find the security safe with the money. Then we can decide what to do with Ana. I'll meet you later, okay? Love you."

"Love you, Catfish."

Sneakers squeak across the floor, and then the door slams.

You aren't sure if you heard correctly. It seems like Nick is **in on the plan**. Your **mind wanders** to that first phone call you got from him, and then to your first meeting with Betty. What other clues did you miss? Did they say anything that would have indicated they were working together? You want to demand answers from your cousin, but all you can do is try to open your eyes. Pain ripples through the back of your head and down your neck when you try to move.

"Don't struggle, Kiddo," Nick says. "I'm **with you** now."

If you think that Nick is reminding you that he is guarding you and that you have no chance of escaping, go to **page 147**.

If you think that Nick is saying that he is going to help you, go to **page 148**.

Nick is reminding you that he is guarding you and that you have no chance of escaping. *Of course*, you think bitterly. He is with Cat. But it doesn't matter. You couldn't escape now even if you wanted to. Your head throbs, and you feel sick and dizzy. You groan, wincing and holding the back of your head.

"I need to make sure I don't have a concussion," you say. "I might need to go to the hospital."

"It's that bad, huh?" Nick looks warily in the direction of the door. "Listen, we don't have time to take you to the hospital. I know you're in a lot of pain, but listen to me carefully. We have to think of a plan before it's too late."

Didn't Nick tell Cat he was the one who hit me?

You decide you can't trust him. Still holding your head, you struggle to **stand up**.

Nick tries to stop you. "Not so fast, Kiddo," he says holding you steady.

"Get off of me!" you yell.

"Easy. Let me help you."

"Help me? **Knocking me out** was helpful enough. Thanks for the cracked skull. At least now I know **where your loyalty lies**."

"Will you listen? I told you—I'm **with *you* now**."

Go to **page 148**.

Nick is saying that he is going to help you. But how can you believe him when he is the one who hit you?

"You aren't **with me**," you say coldly. "I heard everything. You're on Cat's **side**. You have been all along."

Nick hangs his head in shame. "Yes, I was. I was wrong. I'm **on your side** now. We're . . . family."

You look at him in disgust. "We haven't been a family for a long time."

You want to tell him how you really feel—how you have felt about your relationship for the last five years. Maybe it is time to **put it all out there in the open**.

Nick grimaces at your words. "I know I haven't been the best cousin in the world—"

"I know how much you love Cat," you interrupt. You don't want to hear his lies and excuses anymore. "I can understand why you would **go against** me. But why my mother—why Ana? After everything she's done for you—" You stop speaking when your **voice cracks**.

Nick can barely **make eye contact**. He looks at the floor. "I was jealous of you," he answers plainly.

"You were jealous . . . of me?"

"Is it so hard to believe?"

"Even though my mother chose to bring *you* to the States instead of *me*?"

Nick walks away from you for a moment. "Don't you get it, Kiddo?" he explodes. "She couldn't bring you here—not with Foster and Cleaning House around. Ana was thinking like an agent all along, protecting you and hiding the money."

"You're lying!" you say, but you start to doubt your feelings.

"Think about it. The watch Cat just took from you? Ana gave it to you because it had some code. By giving you the watch on your eighteenth birthday, she was protecting the fortune. No one else could get to it because you had it and were far away."

"Why wouldn't she just tell me and get it all **out in the open**? Why would she hide all this from me?"

"She loves you. She was protecting you from all this . . . **dirty business**."

You shake your head in disbelief. "So you were **in on this** the whole time? How could you do it?" Then you remember something. "The phone call to bring me here—you planned it with them!"

He sighs and hangs his head as he continues. "At first, Cat and Betty thought you knew something or had some information about the money. But after a while, they decided you were ignorant about the whole thing. So, they waited, sending you on stupid, fake trainings or missions to see if your mother would secretly **get in touch** with you."

You feel like an idiot. Everything—the secret sweeping signal, the messages on Facebook, and the meetings—were all a sham. You were so eager to believe that Betty needed your help that you ignored what your **gut was telling you** all along.

"The tracking device," you mutter, remembering how Betty wanted to **keep close tabs** on you. You thought she was protecting you. It was all part of her performance.

*She **put on a great show**, and I **fell for it all** . . .*

You turn to your cousin. "And you," you say, stabbing a finger at Nick. "Why did you do it?"

"I thought if I agreed to their plan, a beautiful woman would love me, I'd be rich, and I'd end up being the hero. After I helped Cat and Betty trick you and find the fortune, I was going to **swoop in** and save your mother. Really. For **what it's worth**, Ana has no idea I'm involved."

"Then, you must know where Betty is hiding her."

Nick shakes his head, ashamed. "I wish I did. They knew better than to tell me. They were afraid I'd let her go before they found the money. They weren't going to **fill me in** until *after* they had the code to **crack open** the safe."

You try to **push your emotions aside** so you can think clearly—like a detective. "Cat and Betty have the watch now, which has the combination to the safe. But they still don't know where the safe is hidden, right?" You look hopeful.

Nick sighs. "Too late. I think Ana might have already told Cat and Betty where it is. Because of the **selfie**."

"What?"

"Cat showed Ana the photo as proof that she'd captured you. If Ana knew you'd been taken, she'd **fold** and reveal where the safe was hidden. Ana is tough, but she's not that tough."

You remember your angry expression when the photo was taken—your desperate outstretched hand as you tried to block Cat's phone, your face twisted in discomfort. The caption on the photo read: "Look who's being replaced." You should have realized something was **off** when Nick seemed surprised that Cat mentioned a Facebook photo. She never posted it. It was all an excuse to get a shot of you to show your mother.

"Oh my God. My mother thinks *I've* been kidnapped," you say to yourself in realization.

"You were Ana's **weak spot**, Kiddo. And now you have to find her fast," Nick says hurriedly. "There's not much time before Cat and Betty find Foster's money."

The only question you still have unanswered is about the silver ring with the green stone that you found in the washing machine at the Laundromat—and the nagging feeling you had about it. "One last question. Did my mother ever wear any jewelry?"

Nick scratches his chin. "I think so. A ring."

"Describe it for me."

"Hmm. It was silver ring with a jade stone in it."

You nod. "That was Ana's. Betty had it in the Laundromat where I first met her," you say gravely. "Do you know where Betty lives?"

"I've **dropped her off** in front of her apartment building before, but she always had an excuse about why I couldn't go inside."

You think through a plan: How will you **figure out** which apartment Betty lives in? **Knock on** every door? The neighbors would get suspicious. Even if you found out which apartment was hers, how would you get inside?

"What does the apartment building look like?"

"It has big, fancy windows," Nick says thoughtfully. "Balconies, too. Nicely constructed ones actually." As a window washer and construction worker, Nick was always admiring architecture.

"Do you have any work uniforms here?" An idea is forming in your head.

"Yeah, I think so."

"Do you have one that will fit me?"

"Well . . . " he starts to say, comparing your slim frame to his muscular one.

"It doesn't matter. I'll wear it anyway."

Go to **page 152.**

When you get to Betty's apartment building, you let Nick **do the talking**. He gains the trust of the lobby manager, convincing him that you are window washers. At first, the man is hesitant, but he eventually gives you and Nick access to the roof.

On the roof, Nick shows you how to use the equipment. He looks like he is **in his element**. Meanwhile, you are a **nervous wreck**. You can feel your knees shaking.

"What's our plan again?" he asks.

"You'll ride the moving platform and wash the windows until you find the right apartment. Watch for **telltale signs** that it's Betty's place. Then you'll **climb inside** and let me in—hopefully all before Betty and Cat get back."

"Are you sure you can handle this?" Nick says, pointing to the metal harnesses. Although you won't be hanging from the roof like he will, he has insisted you wear a harness for safety. "You aren't afraid of heights, are you?"

"Of course not," you lie. You are terrified of heights, but you **keep it to yourself**. "Besides, you're going to be doing most of the work."

Holding your breath, you carefully lower Nick down over the ledge of the roof. You stop when he gives you the **thumbs up**. He starts on the top floor first, methodically washing the windows from left to right. When he finishes a row of windows, he nods at you, and you slowly lower him down another floor. By the time he is halfway down, you begin to have doubts about your plan. How can you be sure your mother is in Betty's apartment? Even if she is, how can you be sure Nick will be able to see her through the window? What if the **curtains are drawn**?

"David!"

You almost don't recognize your real name coming out of Nick's mouth. "What is it?"

"I think I see something," Nick says. He tugs on the pulley holding up the platform.

"Are you sure?" you call out.

He tugs harder, pulling you toward the edge of the ledge.

"Don't **let me down**, Nick!"

If you are warning Nick not to pull too hard and make you fall, go to **page 154**.

If you don't want Nick to be wrong about your mother being there, go to **page 156**.

You are warning Nick not to pull too hard and make you fall. You brace the rope with your whole body, hoping it will **hold**. "Fine. I'll lower you down more," you call out. "But stop yanking on the ropes. I'll **tip over**."

"What? I only pulled on the rope one time to get your attention."

All of a sudden, your smartphone vibrates in your pocket. You glance at the screen.

Turn around.

Someone tackles you from behind, throwing you to the ground just inches from the edge of the roof. The fall nearly **knocks the wind out of you**, but you manage to roll away from the ledge. You scramble to get up, but your attacker is **two steps ahead**. A rope goes around your neck. You claw at it, trying to loosen its grip on your windpipe. Gasping for air, you **turn around** and face your assailant. Cat stares back at you with an **icy glare**. With one hard jerk of the rope, she spins you back around. When you refuse to go down, she **knees** you in the back. You finally topple over, slumping to the ground. If she can pry your hands away, the rope will get a better grip—and you will certainly be strangled to death. You try to scream for help but only manage to cough and sputter.

Out of nowhere, the rope slackens. Cat has miraculously let you go. It doesn't make sense. Your eyes water, and your throat burns. You cough and gasp. To your surprise, you see Nick wrestling Cat to the ground. He has managed to rip the rope out of her hands. They struggle, but eventually Nick gains control and pins Cat down.

"I thought we were partners!" she screams at your cousin.

"**Partners in crime**? Not anymore, Catfish." Nick tosses you the rope, and you **crouch down** to tie her hands behind her back.

Once she is secured, you demand, "Which apartment is my mother in?"

"Screw you," Cat snaps back.

You check her pockets and find a set of keys. One of them says "916" on them. "Found it."

Nick **picks up** Cat and throws her over his shoulders. "Not so tough now, are you?" he says to her.

Then the three of you **head down** to apartment #916. When you open the door, you immediately see someone tied to a chair, facing away from you. Nick locks Cat away the hallway closet and runs to the person in the chair.

Nick?" the person exclaims, **turning around**. "**How on earth** did you find me?"

But it isn't Nick she stares at but you.

Go to **page 157**.

You don't want Nick to be wrong about your mother being there. You don't want him to **let you down** and disappoint you. This all just seems **too good to be true**. For the first time, you feel so close, so hopeful. You are worried something will ruin it.

Your **heart pounds** as you carefully lower your cousin down a few more inches until his feet are touching the floor of the balcony. He tugs at the pulleys again to let you know he is fine. Then he starts to knock hard on the window. You can hear him yelling. You want him to be quiet, but you also feel overwhelmed with emotion. You imagine him putting a tiny instrument in the lock and pulling the sliding door to the side.

You stop breathing for a moment, wondering if he has been caught. Minutes pass without a sign. You are about to **give up** when you see him reemerge at the edge of the balcony.

"916!" he shouts at you from below.

You race down the stairs to meet him in the apartment. You don't have much time before Betty and Cat return. When you open the door, you immediately see someone tied to a chair, facing away from you.

You can't **believe your eyes**. *Is it really her?*

Go to **page 157**.

When your mother sees you, she opens her arms and starts sobbing. You and Nick embrace her. The three of you stand there for a long time laughing and crying happy tears.

After you all **get the chance** to **catch your breath**, she stands back and looks at you. "My son!" she cries. "You're a man now."

You nod proudly. You can't believe it has been fifteen years since you have seen each other in person. You know she has been through a lot. She looks like she has aged more than twenty years, and she is even tinier than you remember her. Still, there is that same familiar sparkle in her eyes—one of toughness and strength.

"I'm going to give you two some privacy," Nick says, squeezing your shoulder and pulling out his cell phone. "Meanwhile, I'm going to call the police."

"Thanks, Nick," you say.

You turn to your mother, feeling like a little kid again.

"I'm so proud of you," she says.

"I'm proud of you, too. And I understand everything—why you did what you did."

She nods again, looking at the ground. "It hurt me every day to be separated from you and to not be able to tell you why. I didn't want you to get **mixed up** in all of this."

"I know that now." You feel your eyes water. "But I **let you down**. I let Frida down. I know she was like a daughter to you."

Your mother is silent as you hear faint sirens in the distance. At least the police are arriving, and you and your mother will be safe.

"What will you tell Frida?"

To your surprise, your mother's face brightens and she smiles. "I'll tell Frida that . . . the money is safe."

"But Betty and Cat have my watch." You show her your now naked wrist. There is actually a mark on your skin where the watch once was. You realize that you never really took it off, that you wore it all the time. "And they know where the security safe is," you add. "They can open it with the watch."

"Oh? You mean the safe with the *fake* money?" she says **with a wink**.

"What? Where's the real money then?"

"Back at home. Our home. I've been sending it to you all along."

"There's **no place like home**," you whisper to yourself, remembering the words she said to you—words that were actually clues all this time.

Your mother explains how the symbol in the watch was only there to lead Betty and Cat to the security safe hidden in an office at American University. "I fooled a professor there—one of their accomplices." The watch was just a **planted** clue. The *real* clue was in your mother's message to you all these years.

You shouldn't be too surprised, but you can't stop looking at her with amazement. Your mother really is a detective—and a damn good one at that.

When the police and paramedics finally arrive, you watch proudly as she shows them her badge and explains everything that has happened. Later that day, you watch a security camera video recording of Cat entering an office at American University. Cat has been caught, but Betty is still **on the run**. The police are confident your mother will eventually **track her down**, too. After it was revealed that Betty had **gone rogue**, Cleaning House, Inc. **filled her position** with a new Head of Operations—your mother.

And her first hire? Do you really need a clue?

THE END

You think that you should try to solve this case alone. Nick doesn't seem to believe you. You glare at Cat who sneers back at you with a devilish grin. You want to scream at her, but you know it won't **do any good**. Nick has been **blindsided** by love. It is obvious whose **side he is on**.

"You're on your own now," she whispers to you, smirking. "Good luck finding your mother."

You decide to leave the apartment and walk around the city to **clear your head**. When you get back to the apartment, you can plan your next move.

Go to **page 160**.

It is dark in Nick's apartment when you get home. You **switch on** the lights. You are shocked to find Cat there, rummaging through your suitcase. A pile of your clothes is on the living room floor. "What the hell are you doing?" you demand.

"Shh," she says, putting a finger to her lips and looking toward Nick's bedroom. She dims the light. "Don't **jump to conclusions**. Let me explain."

Your **heart starts to pound**. What does she need to explain? She was clearly rifling through your things. You start walking toward her. "I don't want to have to wake Nick," you threaten.

"I don't either," she says curtly. "And we don't have to. This was just a misunderstanding. I was just trying to clean up around here. When I was clearing the side table, going through the papers **and junk mail**, one of the letters fell in your open suitcase. I was digging around for it."

"That's a lame story," you say.

In the low light, you see Cat's eyes flicker in the direction of the door. Before she **breaks for a run**, you tackle her to the ground. You are a tangle of arms, elbows, and shoulders. You try to wrestle the letter out of her hand, but Cat is fast. She hides the envelope under her body so you can't reach it. Her hand clamps down on your mouth. Desperately, you try to bite her fingers, but, instead of knuckles, you feel something cold and wet on your lips. You taste bitter chemicals and start coughing. Cat is covering your mouth with a rag laced with some kind of drug.

Then, as if **on cue**, Cat the actress starts screaming.

Seconds later, Nick runs out of the bedroom. "**What the hell!**" Nick yells, turning up the light. His eyes are bloodshot.

"Baby!" Cat cries. "He just attacked me." She points at you accusingly.

"Is this true?" Nick asks you accusingly as Cat **jumps into his arms**. He rocks and holds her gently as she covers her face with her hands.

You notice your mother's jade ring on her finger. Did Nick finally propose to her? You can't believe what is happening. Nick **has fallen for her act**.

"I told him to stop—I told him we were engaged now. That you were my fiancée," Cat continues. "But he said he didn't care. He just kept saying I was **turning him on**."

"Wait—" you try to speak. Sick and dizzy from the chemicals in the rag, you sway on your feet. "Nick, don't believe her—"

Without letting you continue, Nick throws you hard against the wall. "I knew I couldn't trust you," he yells, grabbing you by the throat.

You have never seen your cousin so **worked up** before. A vein throbs in his temple, threatening to burst. Spit flies from his mouth. You think he might kill you.

"Is it true?" he demands, his face inches away from yours.

You try to **hold his gaze**, but you are too dizzy to stay focused.

"Answer me!"

"No!" you cry out, coughing and gasping for air. "She's lying, Nick. She's a—"

Before you can answer, his fist smashes into your jaw. You topple over, feeling your body hit the floor with a thud. Soon, the room **spins** above your head. Everything **goes black**.

Go to **page 162**.

When you finally **wake up**, you can hear Nick and Cat's voices whispering over your head. You can't open your eyes or move your body, but you can hear what they are saying.

"Should we call an ambulance?" Nick asks, his voice calmer now.

"I don't think it's necessary. His face is just swollen. He's going to be in a lot of pain when he gets up, but he'll live. I think you should go to the store to get some ice and pain meds. I'll stay with him."

"Are you serious?" Nick says, his anger returning. "After what he tried to do to you? You can't be here alone with him. Go get the ice. I'll **take care of** him."

You don't like **the sound of that**. Is he going to finish what he started? Is he going to kill you this time?

"You sure?" Cat asks. Then there's silence. "Fine. I guess I'll go. Just, um, **give him space**—some **breathing room**." You hear the door slam.

Your eyes **flutter open**, and you whisper, "Nick, please don't kill me. Cat isn't who you think she is. You need to know the truth. She's a—"

"A spy," Nick finishes for you. "She's a spy for Foster. I know, Kiddo. And I'm not **falling for her** anymore."

If you think that Nick is saying that he isn't **in love** with Cat anymore, go to **page 163**.

If you think that Nick is saying that Cat is only pretending to be **in love** with him, go to **page 164**.

Nick is saying that he isn't **in love** with Cat anymore.

"How is that possible? I've never seen you so happy in your life. You can't just **fall out of love** with someone!"

"It's true. I still have feelings for her. But I'm not **falling for her act** anymore."

Go to **page 164**.

Nick is saying that Cat is only pretending to be **in love** with him. He is telling you that he won't let himself be fooled, that he won't **fall for her act** anymore. How did he **figure it out**?

Before you can respond, Nick pulls out an envelope from under his shirt and hands it to you. "Looking for this?"

"How did you—"

"I felt it in the back pocket of her jeans when I was hugging her. I had a feeling **something was up** with her. Detective skills must **run in the family**."

You stare at him in shock.

"To tell you the truth, ever since I proposed to her, I've been a little bit more paranoid than usual. I was suspicious she was **cheating on me**. So I started going through her pockets and looking through her phone when she wasn't around. I'm not proud of it, I admit. Well, this morning I found the envelope in the pocket of her jacket. When I saw it was addressed to Foster, I remembered what you said about Ana's case, so I put it back in your suitcase. Cat must have noticed it was missing and was looking for it."

Holding your breath, you tear open the envelope he gives you. "There's an address here."

"Let me see," he says, taking it out of your hand. Then he nods.

"Nick," you start to say. "Listen, I'm so—"

"Wait," he interrupts you. "Me first. I have to **come clean** about something. I've been **holding out on you**. I think I may have had some important information all along."

"Okay, I'm listening."

"A few days before Ana disappeared I went to her apartment without calling her first like I usually do. When I walked in, the couch had been moved. I asked her if she needed help moving it back, but she **brushed me off**. After that, she started acting strangely. She was really nervous. She asked if I was hungry and pointed to the food on the stove. Then she said she'd be **right back**. I didn't **think twice** about it."

You shake your head in disbelief. "She must have been hiding something behind the couch. I can't believe it. You should have told me all this sooner."

"At the time, I didn't think anything of it because your mother always moved furniture around when she cleaned. Then, I guess I forgot about it. I've had other **things on my mind**."

"Like pleasing Cat."

"Proposing to Cat," he corrects you. "I tried to ignore the **red flags**—and it was easy for a while. Whatever Cat has done, I still care for her."

You don't know what to say. You feel angry at what your cousin has done, but you also feel sad for him.

He looks at you mournfully. "Even though I haven't had a **change of heart** about Cat, I've **changed my mind** about her," he says. "How can I **make it up** to you?"

If you think that Nick feels guilty for not sharing information sooner and now wants to help you, go to **page 166.**

If you think that Nick is telling you that he isn't lying, go to **page 168.**

Nick feels guilty for not sharing information sooner and now wants to help you. **Fair enough**. You will give him the **benefit of the doubt**.

With what he just told you, you know now your mother was hiding something in her apartment. When she realized she was being followed, she took her stash and hid it somewhere else. All you need to do now is find whatever it was she was hiding and contact Foster to lure him to you.

Nothing to it.

"I think I know where to start," you tell Nick, waving the envelope in the air. "This looks like an invoice of some kind to Cleaning House. Someone must have stolen it and mailed it to Foster. It might be one of my mother's clients. The only problem is . . . "

The only problem is Nick's sneaky girlfriend, Cat. She has been following you and your cousin for months. You look at Nick for a moment. She **preyed on** his innocence. He was madly **in love** with her. Can he **turn the tables on her** and play her game?

"You're worried about Cat," Nick says, **reading your mind.**

"Can you still pretend you love her?" you ask him. "To **throw her off** my trail?

He looks at you with sadness. "I don't have to pretend. But what do I say when she comes back, and you're gone?"

"Go to the hospital and call her from there. Tell her you had to take me to the emergency room. Just don't make her suspicious. She can't know anything."

Nick winces. He points at your jaw and touches his own. "Yeah, sorry about the face."

You almost forgot about your swollen, bruised face. "It hurts like hell, you idiot, but you had to make it look real. Actually, on **second thought**, maybe it was **a tad** too real," you say with a slight grin. Smiling has never hurt this much before.

"You believe Ana took whatever she was hiding to that address?" Nick asks, pointing at the envelope.

"I won't know until I **check it out**," you answer, grabbing your jacket. You make sure you have the address and your watch with you before you run out the door.

"Good luck, Detective Dave!" your cousin shouts as you leave.

Yeah, I like the sound of that.

Go to **page 169**.

Nick is telling you that he isn't lying. But you aren't going to **fall for his lies** again. Your cousin can't be trusted. The only person in the family he **looks out for** is himself.

"I know you're just **making things up**. I don't believe you." You get up and **head toward** the door. You have to escape before Cat returns. It is **you against them**.

Nick blocks your way. "What is there left to **make up**? I confessed already. I admit I was stupid, Kiddo. Please believe me. What can I do or say to make things better between us?"

"Nothing," you answer. You glare at your cousin until the dizziness and pain forces you to **sit down** again.

"Besides, look at you. You're not well. You need me now."

"I can do this **on my own**."

Nick ignores you. "**Come on**. Let me **make it up to you** by helping you find Ana."

Go to **page 166**.

You stand nervously outside of a brick row house in Capitol Hill. You knock on the door. At first there is no answer. You knock again, louder.

Finally, you hear someone walking up to the door. It opens to reveal a woman in her early twenties. The woman looks familiar. You have seen her before. An image **comes to mind**: the young girl in the costume in the photograph.

"May I help you?" she asks.

"Yes, um, do you receive services from Cleaning House, Inc.?"

"Yes, I hire them to clean my house sometimes," the woman answers. She looks worried. She must have no idea who you are or why you are here. "They clean while I'm at work. Why? Is there a problem?"

"Who is it?" a male voice calls out from inside the house.

"I'm sorry," she says. "This is kind of a bad time. I'm a little busy right now. I have company—family visiting from **out of town**. Can you come back another time?"

She goes to close the door, but you stop it with your foot. "Wait," you say, trying to **get to the point**. "You know my mother. My mother is Ana."

"Ana," she whispers. "What about Ana?"

"Frida, Ana was here in your house."

She covers her mouth with her hand. She is shocked to hear her own name and your mother's name spoken in the same sentence.

"Who's there?" you hear the man say impatiently. He comes to the door and glares at you. You stare at the man and see a glimmer of recognition. It is Frederick Foster.

"Oh my God," he says, realizing who you are.

"What's going on?" Frida asks.

Without answering her, the man starts pacing around the house, looking under furniture and inside cabinets. "No, it's mine. I have to get to it first," he mutters to himself.

Frida follows Foster as he tears through the rooms.

"Frida, your father is looking for a safe with his money in it," you explain.

"What?" Frida cries, shocked.

"Well, actually it belongs to you now. My mother hid it from him. The money is why he kidnapped her, and why he's here now."

"Tell me where it is, David!" Foster yells.

He grabs a hammer from a drawer and raises it high in the air. You wonder briefly whether he is going to attack you. But then he swings the heavy tool against the wooden cabinets, splintering the wood. He will **tear down** the house to find the hidden fortune.

"If you ever want to see your mother alive, tell me where it is! Tell me now!"

"My mother first—tell me where she is first."

"This isn't a game," he says, ripping drawers out of cabinets and doors off of their hinges.

"Please, Dad," Frida exclaims. "Why are you doing this? I thought you were done. You promised me you had **turned over a new leaf**."

"Foster, where is she?" you demand.

Foster looks at his daughter. His face is full of pain.

"Dad," she pleads more.

Finally, he throws down the hammer. "She's in the trunk of my car," he says with resignation. "I brought her here a few hours ago to make her tell me where the money was, but she wasn't talking."

The idea of your poor mother imprisoned in the trunk of his car **sends you into a rage**. You lunge for him, but Foster is too strong. He pushes you off but not before he grabs your watch and throws it far across the room.

From the **corner of your eye**, you see Frida pick up the watch. "Push the button on the side!" you instruct her.

To your surprise, she does.

Within a few minutes, red and blue flashing lights can be seen through the window. The police have Frida's house surrounded.

Using a megaphone, one of the officers orders Foster to come out with **his hands up**. Foster **doesn't bother** to **put up a fight**.

Once in handcuffs, Foster turns to look at you one last time. It is a look of bitterness and awe. "I just don't **get it**. I looked everywhere. I made sure I checked every room, looked inside every **nook and cranny** . . ."

"You're right, you did look everywhere—**everywhere but the kitchen sink**," you say with a grin.

If you are saying that Foster looked everywhere but not in the right place, go to **page 172**.

If you are saying that Foster should have looked in the kitchen sink, go to **page 174**.

Foster looked everywhere but not in the right place.

You wait until Betty arrives at the scene. Then you take both her and Frida to the kitchen. You point to a framed print on the wall above the breakfast table.

Home Sweet Home

"There's **no place like home**, right Dorothy?" you say to Frida.

Betty reaches up and slowly takes the framed print down from the wall. She turns it over on the table and lays it flat. On the back of the thick wooden frame, in the lower right-hand corner is an unusual **cubby space**. You open it, revealing a small, hidden compartment. When Frida looks inside, she gasps. Instead of money there are tiny jewels—numerous, sparkling diamonds.

Your mother truly was a detective. She hid the fortune in a place she thought only you would be able to **figure out**—because of the Mayan symbol inside your watch. You knew what it meant all along. It was the symbol for "home." When you saw the print in the kitchen earlier, it suddenly **all clicked**.

Your mother is alive but in shock from being **stuffed in the trunk** of Foster's car. As the paramedics load her on a stretcher, you grab her hand. She squeezes your hand in return. The paramedics tell you she is going to the hospital for observation, and you can see her as soon as you are done being interviewed by the police.

As the ambulance drives away, you see a car **pull up** to the curb. The officers try to **wave them away**, but you see it is Nick. You are surprised to see Cat with him. You alert the officers and motion for your cousin and Cat to come over. Cat looks genuinely concerned and holds Nick's hand. She is still wearing your mother's jade ring.

Hours later, the police have **sectioned off** the entire block with yellow tape to **keep out** curious bystanders. You and Frida stand outside, still in shock, explaining what you know to the detectives.

After the incident, Cat accepts a **plea bargain**. In exchange for a **lighter sentence**, she reveals the rest of Foster's illegal activities. She is **put on** probation for a year and placed **under house arrest**. Foster, on the other hand, receives twenty-five years in prison.

Despite Cat's antics, Nick is still very much **in love** with her, and surprisingly, Cat starts to show genuine interest in him. She insists that she has never met a man who still loved her **no matter what** bad choices she has made. To her credit, Cat gives back the jade ring. With Cat under house arrest, Nick jokes that it will be easy to **keep an eye on her** now.

The story about your mother's kidnapping and your novice detective work receives national attention. For months you, your mother, Cat, Nick, and Frida are called in for TV interviews and appearances. The public seems especially fascinated by your mother—the housekeeper-turned-spy. However, your mother isn't that interested **in the limelight**. After much debate, she decides to retire from investigative work. She signs up for archaeology and ancient language courses at the local university. Frida offers your mother a portion of the fortune to pay for classes.

When the media attention finally **dies down**, you decide to return home and finish school. You are now studying criminal justice. Betty promises you a job with Cleaning House, Inc. after you graduate. You now feel like you have two homes instead of one. For now, though, you feel happy being away from all the excitement in D.C.

As for your crime novel habit, you aren't reading much of those books lately ever since you changed **majors**. Anyway, you could probably write a crime or mystery novel of your own. After all, you are a **seasoned** detective now.

THE END

Foster should have looked in the kitchen sink. The joke you make doesn't **go down well**. Foster just glares at you. He knows you are being sarcastic.

"I don't know how you did it," he grumbles as the cops lead him away with his arms handcuffed behind his back.

Frida looks at you with **tears rolling down** her cheeks. She has just lost her father again. You feel tremendous sadness for her. Unlike you and your mother, Frida and her father may never be together again.

"Frida," you say to her gently. "Your father looked everywhere, but he **missed a spot**. Come, I'll show you."

Go to **page 172**.

The **fortune-teller**'s advice encourages you to think about your life. It is true that you have had a bad attitude about your family and your past. You blamed your mother for leaving you. But the truth is your mother has always been supportive. She paid for you to go to college. If you eventually become a well-respected doctor, you will have her to thank.

And yet you wonder . . . Your mother was always the one to encourage you to **follow your dreams**. As a kid, your dream was to be a detective. You remember how your mother would play along and give you riddles to solve. Whenever she gave you a clue, and you didn't understand it, she would explain it this way: "Words and phrases often have **double meanings**. The *true* meaning depends on the situation. Don't just look or listen to what the literal meaning is."

"You mean like a secret code?"

"Yes, just like a secret code. Use all the clues around you, not just what people say. Look at how they say something and where and when they say it."

As you think about this, you gently touch the watch your mother gave you as a gift. Your mother had an inscription put on the back of the watch that you never quite understood before. You turn over your watch and read the etched words.

Never forget what makes you tick.

If you think that the inscription means to stay calm and not let things make you angry, go to **page 176**.

If you think that the inscription means to never forget about what truly makes you happy in life, go to **page 177**.

The inscription on the watch means to stay calm and not let things make you angry.

"Never forget what makes you tick." You think about the words and sniff. *That's easy for her to say.* There is so much you should be **ticked off** about.

But something doesn't seem right. You read the words again. You wonder if there might be another meaning to the inscription. What else ticks in real life? You look at your watch again, observing one of the hands move, counting and **ticking off** the seconds. Of course, your watch ticks. The gears and machinery inside it give it life and make it work.

You think about your own life. What makes *you* tick? What **makes up** who you are? Sure, you are **made up** of cells, tissues, and organs; that is you physically. But what *really* makes you, well, you?

Go to **page 177**.

[CHAPTER FIVE]

~ What Makes You Tick?

THE INSCRIPTION MEANS to never forget about what truly makes you happy in life. You repeat the words in your head. "Never forget what makes you tick."

Suddenly, you realize what does make you happy in life: solving mysteries. For years you have been denying your true self. You don't want to be an eye doctor. You want to solve puzzles, look for evidence, and analyze the expressions of suspects to see if they are telling you the truth. This is what really **makes you tick**. You want to **follow in your mother's footsteps**.

What next? You look at your watch. It is now fifteen minutes behind. For such a valuable watch, it is quite unreliable. You can hear your mother's voice in your head: "Don't forget to **wind it up**." But what use is a watch that you have to wind so often?

This watch is just as reliable as she is.

Thank goodness for your smartphone. It always **keeps the right time.** You see it is five o'clock.

"You'll understand when the time is right," your mother used to say. She first said this to you on your eighteenth birthday, that horrible day when you found out she was going to bring Nick to the

States instead of you. What did she mean when she said those words? You look at your watch, remembering how other people have shown such great interest in it. You sigh. Maybe you should listen to your mother **for once**.

Carefully, you twist the knob on the side of the watch. When the second hand is on the correct minute, you wait for something to happen. You tap the glass face. Nothing.

You try an experiment. You place both the watch and smartphone side by side. Watching the seconds tick away, you soon notice your watch falling behind. You twist the knob again, matching the watch to the correct time on your smartphone, and wait.

Click.

It is a tiny sound, but you hear it. Now you press gently on the glass cover and it **pops opens**. You examine the intricate parts inside, a cluster of tiny gears connected by even tinier screws and bolts. You can't even begin to understand it. What you do know is that the parts fit together and work as a system to **tell time**.

As you observe the delicate machinery stir and move, you see something. Tiny shapes are engraved on the metal gears. To the **casual observer**, they might just look like simple scratches. But you know better. When you wind the watch again, the gears move closer, aligning the shapes and marks into a Mayan symbol that only you and your mother would know. The symbol that appears inside your watch means "home."

Now you feel like you are closer to solving this mystery. Rather than following Betty's next **lead**, you decide to go back to Nick's apartment. Is it time to **come clean** to Nick?

If you aren't sure it is a good idea to tell Nick anything yet, go to **page 134**.

If you are confident it is the right thing to do to tell Nick the truth, go to **page 160**.

You should tell Nick everything and stop **keeping him in the dark**. Nick is your family **after all**. He deserves to know the truth. Although you haven't been close for the past five years, he has changed and **grown up**. This is your chance to **make up** for all those years of silence. It will feel good to tell the truth—to get **everything off your chest**.

"Actually, Nick," you say with a sigh. "We need to talk." Nick's smile disappears as you put your hand on his shoulder.

"I don't like the sound of this," he says softly. "Is this about Ana?"

You nod. Then you **take a deep breath**. "And Cat."

Nick moves uncomfortably on the couch. "My Catfish?"

You look him in the eyes. "Whatever I tell you right now, I need you to trust me."

Nick nods silently.

"I'm working for an undercover detective agency. Betty Rogers, the woman who works with my mother, asked me to help collect evidence and **follow up on leads**. They have a suspect named Frederick Foster. My mother used to work for him. Betty seems to think Foster might lead us to her."

He gives you a serious look, nodding his head with concern. Then he laughs and slaps you on the back. "**Nice one**, Kiddo. I **get it**. You're trying to **pull a fast one** on me."

You look at him seriously. "I'm not kidding. You can ask Cat."

Nick's smile disappears. "Cat knows about this?"

"She's been **tailing** me, keeping track of me around town."

"I don't understand . . . " he says, shaking his head. "Why?"

A **lump forms in your throat** again. "Cat isn't who she says she is, Nick. Foster—the man who might have taken my mother—hired Cat to spy on us. She's one of his agents."

Nick looks at you for a long time, waiting for you to tell him it is a joke; you wish you could. When you shake your head, he turns away. "It can't be true," he insists. "What Cat and I have is real. I don't know why you'd want to—"

Just then, you hear someone at the door. Cat has decided to come back after all. "Why don't you ask her yourself?"

"Ask me what?" Cat says happily, her arms full of shopping bags as usual. She walks in the living room, puts the bags down beside your suitcase on the floor and comes right over to Nick to kiss him on the cheek.

"Tell Nick the truth, Cat," you say, your **heart beating fast**. "Tell him that you know I'm not actually Kevin. Tell him that you know who kidnapped my mother and that you're working for the man."

Cat, the actress and spy, puts on a convincingly surprised look. "You're not Kevin?" She looks at Nick with confusion and fear. "What is your friend talking about?"

"Enough with **the act**," you say. "Nick needs to know the truth."

Cat drops her bags and looks at you with narrowed eyes.

"Think about it," you say to your cousin, **breaking the silence**. "Why would I lie to you about all of this, Nick? **What's in it for me**?"

"He's just jealous, Baby," Cat explains. "He wants us to **break up**. He's been trying to **hit on** me since he got here."

"Nick," you say, ignoring Cat. "Do you remember waking up last night?"

Nick is silent.

"Do you remember waking up and coming into the kitchen because you heard people talking? That was Cat and me. She came here late last night to talk to me **in secret**." You take Nick by the shoulders and shake him. "Are **you following me** now?"

If you are asking Nick to go with you somewhere
to have a private conversation, go to **page 181**.

If you are asking Nick if he understands what you
are trying to say, go to **page 182**.

You are asking Nick to go with you somewhere to have a private conversation without Cat's influence. You start walking toward the bathroom, hoping that Nick will follow you. Instead, you **turn around** and see that Cat has walked over to him and grabbed his hand. Helplessly, Nick looks back and forth between the two of you, not sure who to go with.

"He's not going anywhere," Cat says to you coldly. "He loves me, right Nick?"

Nick just stares at her blankly, like a **deer caught in headlights**. It is clear that he is still trying to remember when he woke up in the middle of the night. "Wait, I do remember something," he says finally. His eyes brighten.

"Yes!" you shout, happy to see Nick starting to **follow you**. "Do you remember me telling you to go back to bed?"

Nick nods his head faster. "I remember hearing people whispering by the front door—it sounded like an argument. When I thought I heard Cat's voice, I thought maybe she needed my help. But then I remembered she was supposed to be at her apartment, so I figured I must have been dreaming."

"See? Now you're starting to **follow me**, Nick," you say with growing excitement. "It wasn't a dream."

Go to **page 182**.

You are asking Nick if he understands what you are trying to say. Nick nods seriously. "Yes, I remember now," he says to you. He turns to look at Cat and shakes his head. "And I'm tired of the lies."

"Listen, Nick . . ." you start to say, a **lump in your throat**. It is the first time you have ever seen your cousin look so unsure about himself.

"Just stop," he says. He then turns away, walks into the bathroom, and slams the door behind him.

You stare at the closed door. Did you do the right thing by telling Nick the truth just now? After everything that has happened over the last few days, you may have lost his trust and confidence. Is it too late to fix your relationship, or is this your time to **have a go** at it again?

If you think that you should try harder to make Nick understand, go to **page 183**.

If you think that you should try to solve this case alone, go to **page 159**.

You should try harder to make Nick understand. You should **have a go** at convincing him that what you did was **in his best interest**.

When you try to go after Nick, Cat stops you. "I thought I could trust you," she says angrily. "I thought we **had a deal**—no **blowing my cover**. Haven't you learned yet, Detective? Agents have to have complete trust in each other to work together."

"We don't work together, Cat."

Cat walks to the apartment door and turns around, her hand poised on the doorknob. "You've **double-crossed me** just like Foster did. You'll regret this."

From inside the bathroom, you can hear Nick yelling and throwing things. The news must have really **broken his heart**. But as much as it hurts now, you know you did the right thing. Cat is wrong. You didn't **double-cross** her. You just **came clean** to your family. *Family first.* **When it comes down to it**, family members are the only ones you can trust.

"Cat, please," you say, trying to reason with her. "**See it my way**."

"I'm done **playing nice**. You'll need my help sooner than you think. And when you do, I'll remember what you did here tonight." Then Cat strides out and slams the door behind her.

Moments later, the bathroom door creaks open. Nick looks like he is **in shock**. "Why didn't I see it before?" he says, groaning. "Why didn't I **see through** her, Kiddo? And you—I never thought you'd lie to me." Nick gives you a miserable glance. His shoulders are slumped and his eyes are red from crying. "I mean, I'm glad you're **coming clean** now, but why didn't you tell me the truth from the beginning? Cat hiding something from me is one thing, but you . . . "

You try to remind him of the time you warned him about Cat, but he keeps going.

"But you know what? That's in the past now. We've both made mistakes. What's important is that we're family. We're all we have right now—all Ana has."

"I'm sorry you had to **find out** this way," you say. "I didn't tell you because I wanted to keep you safe."

He smiles and nods. "It's okay, Kiddo. We're **in this together** now." He gives you a hug. "Listen," he continues. "I know what you think of me. I know you're still mad about Ana bringing me here instead of you all those years ago. I'm going to **make it up** to you, I promise. I'm going to **make things right**."

"I believe you." Nick has never looked more serious and sincere in his life.

"Hey, look," he says, pointing to some bags by the front door. "Cat forgot her stuff."

You remember her shopping bags on the bus ride to Nick's apartment and how she acted strange when you looked inside them. You both run over to the bags and dig through them. At first, you don't see anything except new clothes, but then you see something underneath the blouses and skirts.

"What do we have here?" Nick holds up a bodysuit with a long tail and a mask with cat ears. "Cat's not just a spy—she's **Cat Woman**!" He gives you a mischievous look. "Hey, maybe you should keep it, man. You can wear it the next time you **go undercover**."

You laugh at Nick's attempt to **lighten the atmosphere**. "I don't think so," you say, **rolling your eyes**. It all seems so ridiculous, but you are interested in Cat's reason for buying the funny costume and leaving it here.

"Where did she buy this thing?" Nick asks curiously, looking for the receipt in the bag. "Victoria's Secret?" He seems to be a little too interested in the cat costume.

The mood is broken when your phone vibrates in your pocket. You see that it is Betty.

> Good news. We may have found the address to Foster's apartment. Wait at home for our signal at three o'clock.

You are **on the heels** of Foster now. The **stakes are higher than ever**. You know you can't waste time or make mistakes. You look at Nick who is still examining the cat costume with fascination. Should you just **show up** at the apartment with him? No, you decide. You need to have complete trust between you and the other people on your team. Cat was right about that.

Hoping for the best, you write back.

> I'm glad you've found the apartment. By the way, I need to tell you that I finally told my cousin about the mission. It was getting too hard to **live a lie**. Anyway, I think he might be able to help us.

At first, Betty doesn't respond. You start to worry that she has lost all trust in you. Then, around three o'clock, there is a knock at Nick's door. On the doorstep is a brown box. When you open the package, you find two uniforms that say "Bomb Squad" on the back.

"Nick!" you yell to get his attention. "Are you ready for your first mission?" When he doesn't answer you, you **look up** and see him nodding excitedly, the cat mask teetering on his face.

Inside the package, you see a typed note. You open it.

> I disagree with your decision to involve your cousin but a good detective needs to **go with his gut**. Just make sure you **keep an eye on him**. This won't be easy for either of you. -B

If you think that Betty wants you to keep Nick out of trouble, go to **page 186**.

If you think that Betty wants you to watch Nick's every move, go to **page 190**.

Betty wants you to keep Nick out of trouble. You smile to yourself as you watch Nick **march in place**. He promises to **take your orders** like a soldier **under your command**. Maybe working with Nick won't be all that bad.

By five o'clock, you and Nick are wearing bomb squad uniforms and dark sunglasses, riding in a black van on the way to Foster's apartment. Betty is in the driver's seat, taking you through the main streets of Washington, D.C. Sitting next to you, your cousin is grinning like a kid on Christmas Day. You, **on the other hand**, are nervous. Your palms sweat and your mouth is dry. If only you could have the same 'I could care less' attitude as your cousin. He always makes everything seem like a fun, effortless adventure. You are also worried about Cat. She left the apartment clearly unhappy with how things **turned out**. She said that you would need her help soon. What did she mean? Was she threatening you?

"So, Betty, are we going to get real guns?" Nick asks, his eyes big with excitement.

"I don't give guns to inexperienced agents," Betty answers. "Besides, I told you already what you're going to do. **Stick to the plan**." She eyes Nick sternly in the rearview mirror.

"Oh, well, I don't need a gun anyway," Nick boasts. He then rolls up the sleeve of his uniform and pats his arm muscle. "I have a **big gun** right here."

You give Nick a stricken look.

"Sorry, Kiddo, but you'd have to spend a couple years at the gym first to **catch up** to my **swag**." He kisses his own bicep muscle.

Betty **rolls her eyes** but manages a small chuckle. You breathe a **sigh of relief**. You are starting to see what Nick is good at. You may **have the brains**, but Nick seems to **have a way with women**. He is charming and funny. Your preparedness and organizational skills **pale in comparison** to Nick's positive attitude and confidence. You wonder if these traits will help you if you get into trouble. Maybe your cousin will be a good **sidekick** after all.

Soon, Betty **turns down** a narrow alley and **pulls up** behind a tall, modern apartment building. She parks and then **turns around** in her seat to face you.

"Let's review our plan. I'm going to call the manager of the apartment building and say there is a bomb somewhere in the building. When you hear the alarm go off, you'll walk right in like you know exactly what you're doing. If someone questions you, tell them there is an emergency. Make it believable, guys."

"That's easy," Nick mutters, with a hint of bitterness. "Just be like my ex-girlfriend. She could fool anyone."

Betty turns to look at you. She seems to sense your nervousness. "David, I need you to **keep your cool**. We won't have a lot of time before the real Bomb Squad will be called in. Work carefully but work fast."

"He's just worried I'm going to **show him up**," Nick jokes.

You give him a look. *Enough already. This isn't a game.*

"David, you'll have just a few minutes to look for clues once you're inside. If the door to Foster's apartment is locked, you can unlock it with the tools inside your bomb squad backpacks—"

"Cool!" Nick interrupts, grabbing a backpack and looking inside.

Betty turns to your cousin. "Nick, your only job is to stand by the door of the apartment and **keep watch**. Can you handle that?"

Nick nods, although he seems more interested in the bomb squad gear. "Whoa!" he exclaims, inspecting a device with a wire sticking out of it.

"You know you aren't actually going to use that **bomb detonator**, right?"

"Aw, man," Nick says, disappointed. "You mean if that Foster guy comes back, I can't just **blow him up**?"

Betty **gives you a look**. *I told you so*, she seems to be saying.

"Nick," Betty says loudly to get your cousin to **pay attention**, "you're going to need a signal word or phrase you can yell to David if you see someone coming. Can you think of one?"

You are afraid to hear his idea. "How about Kiddo?" he suggests.

"How original," you say dryly.

After gathering and checking your equipment, you signal to Betty that you are ready.

"Okay, guys. **Look alive**," Betty says. "Remember, I'm right outside if you need me."

You look at your watch with its emergency button and nod with understanding.

As you walk up to the front of the building, you hear an alarm start beeping. You stop and observe from the side of the building as hundreds of people walk out and gather in groups.

"**Game on**," Nick says, walking confidently to the entrance. You follow him as he walks right through the crowds of people, yelling in a loud voice, "Everyone, please **stand back**. We need everyone at a safe distance. Please stand on the other side of the street and **clear a path**. We will inform you when it is safe to reenter the building. **Move it**, people! We **don't have all day**."

Not bad, Nick, not bad.

When the building is clear, you run up the stairs to Foster's apartment, #501. The door is locked. With your **heart pounding**, you pull out a metal tool from your bag and **jimmy** the lock—the way Betty showed you. The door swings open.

You and Nick stand there for a moment, waiting for someone to confront you, but the room is completely silent and still. You walk through the apartment and check all the rooms and closets.

"All clear. Wait here," you tell Nick, motioning for him to stand by the front door. "I'll look for clues and **take pictures**. If anyone **shows up**, just yell: 'Do you see the bomb in there?' That'll be our signal."

Nick nods and doesn't argue.

You **take a look** in each room of the apartment. There are dirty dishes in the kitchen sink. The bed in the bedroom is unmade. There are papers lying around all over the place. *Looks like he left in a hurry.*

You rifle through the papers, mostly stacks of packages and mail. Several of the envelopes have on them the official label of American University, one of your mother's cleaning sites. All of these letters have been sent from an American University professor named Dr. Khan. They are addressed to a name you recognize.

Frederick Foster

You slip one of the envelopes in your pocket and tell yourself not to lose it.

You go to the living room area and explore further. You find a desk with a laptop. The screen is on and open to a Facebook page belonging to someone named "Dorothy Dixon." The profile picture is of a young woman posing in a cat costume. Because she is wearing a mask that covers her head, you can't see her face very clearly. You try to look at the rest of her Facebook page. She has over a thousand likes and hundreds of comments from people. Several people have written: "Great job," "Encore!" and "Can't wait for the next one." The last comment reads: "You'll **be a star** one day!"

You study the page. The woman is in a show where she is **playing** a cat. You look at some of the papers on the desk. You notice several colorful **brochures**. Picking one up, you see an advertisement for a show called *CATS* at the National Theater.

The cat costume in Cat's shopping bag **comes to mind**. Before Cat **stormed out** of Nick's apartment, she must have been **letting the cat out of the bag**.

If you think that Cat was simply expressing how angry she was, go to **page 191**.

If you think that Cat was revealing information to you, go to **page 192**.

Betty wants you to watch Nick's every move. But that is impossible. You are **no match** for Nick. Even **on your best day**, you could never **keep up** with him physically.

You look over at Nick, who is eagerly doing push-ups and sit-ups on the ground now. You **clear your throat**. "Ahem, Nick?"

Nick **jumps to attention**. He claps his hands together and starts jogging in place. "I'm **pumped**! Just tell me what to do!"

"This is going to be a dangerous mission," you warn him. "We're going to the suspect's home. You're going to have to listen to me, stay close, and follow orders. I know that might be hard for you."

He salutes you. "Yes, sir! I am at your service, SIR!"

You smile to yourself. Maybe it won't be so hard to **keep an eye on** him.

Go to **page 186**.

Cat was simply expressing how angry she was. She threatened you before she left the apartment, right? She has every reason to be **pissed off** because you revealed her identity to Nick. But maybe Cat left the bags behind **on purpose**. Maybe she was **sending you a message**. If so, was it because she was angry or because she wanted to help you somehow?

You look at the Facebook page again. You click through all the photos of Dorothy Dixon. All the pictures are of her in different costumes on stage. Nothing **catches your eye** until you get to the most recent photo. Your **mouth hangs open** in shock. Dorothy is wearing a black cat costume—almost exactly the same style as the cat costume in Cat's shopping bag. It can't just be a coincidence. You click the photo to enlarge it.

Cat, what are you trying to tell me?

Go to **page 192.**

Cat was revealing information to you. You review what you know. Cat was a spy working for Foster. Later, he betrays her. She now has a motive to work against him. Then she comes over to Nick's apartment and leaves a cat costume for you to find—a costume similar to what Dorothy Dixon was wearing in a photo on her Facebook page. Now you find that Facebook page on Foster's laptop, as well as a brochure for a show called *CATS* on his desk. Along with all the other clues you have gathered so far, it finally makes sense: Dorothy Dixon *is* Frida Foster.

Next, you snoop inside the bedroom. You see a chair in the corner of the room against the wall. A pile of nylon ropes and masking tape is stashed under a nightstand. Your hands shake as you touch the chair where your mother might have been tied up. On the other nightstand, you see another laptop. You open it.

Your **knees buckle**, and you almost collapse on the bed when you see the screen. On the browser is a Google search page for "**D-I-Y** Explosives." You look around in a panic, realizing that the room is littered with wires, timers, and plastic casings.

What does Frederick Foster need with a bomb?

Wherever Foster has gone, your mother is most likely with him.

As if **on cue**, you hear Nick yell from the entrance of the apartment, "Ah, do you see any bombs back there?"

"No," you respond. "But it **looks like** Foster has the supplies here to build one." You push the emergency button on your watch.

"Um, are you sure there are no bombs in there right *now*?" Nick yells again, this time, sounding desperate.

Oh, the signal.

"Wait! I do see something back here—a **suspicious package**. Everyone needs to stay out of the area until we disable it," you say out loud.

You grab the two laptops for safekeeping and join Nick at the door. Nick **clears his throat** and points to a big man in a business suit walking down the hallway toward you.

"Please, sir—" you say.

"Steve Rubino," the man announces, waving you off. "I'm the building manager here. What the hell is going on?"

"Mr. Rubino, I'm afraid it's still not safe to be inside the building," you explain, trying to keep your voice from **cracking**. "We received a tip about a bomb in apartment #501."

"Interesting," the building manager answers, still doubtful. "And which department are you with?"

"The Washington D.C. Bomb Squad."

"**You don't say?**" He looks at you with suspicion. "Another so-called Bomb Squad just arrived a minute ago." He points a giant finger down the hall.

A group of men in thick, protective uniforms appears. They organize into two columns and proceed to stop at each apartment door on the floor. One man leads a **bomb-sniffing** dog and another man drives a **remote**-controlled machine on wheels.

Steve grabs you hard enough by the arm to break it. "Tell me who you really are."

Nick looks at you nervously. You decide the only way to avoid a **showdown** with the manager is to pretend you are part of the real Bomb Squad.

If you think that you should yell down the hall to the Bomb Squad, "Finally! We've been waiting for you to **show up!**" go to **page 194**.

If you think that you should yell down the hall to the Bomb Squad, "Finally! We've been waiting for you to **show us up!**" go to **page 195**.

You yell down the hall to the Bomb Squad, "Finally! We've been waiting for you to **show up**!"

The Bomb Squad men look at each other for a moment and then one of them approaches you. "I'm Squad Leader Lt. Lou Burnside. You've been waiting for our team? Are you the first responders?"

You hold out your hand for a handshake, but the squad leader just stares at your outstretched hand. His face is expressionless.

"We're . . . undercover," you blurt out, showing him your fake badge. "Part of the, um, Special Ops Division. We're new—a new undercover **wing** of the department—you should **stop by** for coffee one time. Half an hour ago, we got a tip about a threat here in #501."

The squad leader **squints at you**. "**Brief** me on what you know. Do we have a **live one**?"

"No, um, I don't think so." You have no idea what he means.

He starts **ticking off** a list in rapid fire. "What's the threat? Biological hazards? Chemical reactives? Do we need HAZMAT suits? What's the detonation device?"

"Uh . . . " you say, looking at Nick. *Need a little help here.*

Nick nods and steps in front of you. "Lt. Burnside, it seemed clean. But it's best if you and your officers do another **sweep**. We don't have the equipment as you can see. But I'd forget about the HAZMAT suits and containment chambers—nothing biological or chemical in there. We also didn't find any detonation devices."

You gape **in awe** at Nick's smooth performance. "Yeah, that's right," you add weakly.

Burnside nods curtly and signals his team to prepare. "We'll **take it from here**."

As you walk toward the stairs, you **take one last look** behind you. The Bomb Squad has entered #501. Steve Rubino, the manager, is still standing outside the door, gazing at you with doubt and amazement.

Go to **page 196**.

"Finally! We've been waiting for you to **show us up**," you yell down the hall to the Bomb Squad.

They all look at you in unison.

"Someone **called in** a bomb threat," the biggest man of the group says to you with a scowl, "and we take these things seriously, especially in this city where things can quickly escalate into a terror situation. We don't try to **show people up** in our **line of work**."

I said the wrong thing. "Um . . . " you mutter.

You have read about S.W.A.T. in some of your crime novels. They are usually law enforcement officers called in for the **worst-case scenarios**, like hostage situations or terror attacks. They are **no joke**. And here they are—**the real thing**.

The man introduces himself. "Squad Leader Lt. Lou Burnside," he says impatiently. "Who are you?"

"We're very sorry, Lt. Burnside," you say quickly. "Uh, we didn't realize the severity of the situation. We're the, er, pre-investigation team from the, um, Special Ops Division. Glad to know you have everything **under control**."

"That's not what they told me a second ago," the building manager **jumps in**.

They all turn and stare at you in confusion. "Special Ops Division?" the squad leader says. "I'm not familiar with—"

"It's a new undercover division. Very **hush-hush**," you explain.

Lt. Lou Burnside isn't impressed at all. You are worried he will ask for your badges or call headquarters to verify your story. Luckily, Nick **jumps in**.

"It looks like there's **no time to waste** here. We'll **get out of your hair** now so that you can complete the check." Nick is dragging you by the arm down the hall. "You'll see our reports about this in the morning," he calls out. "**Carry on**, Burnside."

Go to **page 196**.

You and Nick race down the stairs to the basement floor and then out the back entrance of the apartment building to the alley. With screeching tires, Betty's black van **pulls up** beside you. She motions for you to jump inside.

"Was anyone there suspicious?" Betty asks as soon as she accelerates away.

"I don't think so," you respond, looking in the rearview mirror to see if anyone is following you. "I think they believed our story. The real guys are looking for a bomb in Frederick's apartment right now."

"Good," Betty says, with a sigh of relief. "What did you find out?" She **revs up the engine** and **floors it**. The van's tires squeal loudly on the asphalt.

You pull out your phone and the brochure for *CATS*. "I think I know where to look next. And how to **look up** Frida Foster." You show the photos again and explain your theory. "Frida Foster has to be Dorothy Dixon. She's an actress performing in a show at the National Theater," you continue, tapping your finger on the brochure for *CATS*. "There's a performance tonight."

"Huh. So Cat knew about it. That would explain the cat costume," Nick says, pulling it out from where you left it in the back seat. "But why would she leave it with us?"

You have wondered the same thing. You have a weird feeling there is more to the costume than just the show. Cat has something **up her sleeve**.

"Another thing. I also saw a bunch of wires and plastic casings in the apartment," you say.

"Foster is doing some electrical wiring?" Nick asks.

"No," you say grimly. "He might be making a bomb. It's on his computer." You show Betty the two laptops you stole from Foster's apartment.

"Did you get everything you needed from them?"

"I think so. But shouldn't we take the computers to the lab?"

"Too risky at this stage. We need to **toss them**." Betty stops the van at a dumpster and tells you to throw away the computers. "Now we have to get to that show and find Frida before Frederick Foster does. We don't know what he plans to do with a bomb. **In any case**, we can't **take any chances**. If we can get to Frida before he does, then we might be able to convince him to **give himself up**."

She **steps on the gas** and changes lanes.

"Uh-oh. We've got one problem," Nick says, motioning for you and Betty to look in the rearview mirror. "**We have company**."

In the mirror you can see a shiny black sports car with tinted windows following the van a few cars behind you.

"How do you know?" you ask, surprised that your cousin noticed. You can't believe how helpful your cousin has been so far.

"There's only one way to be sure," Betty answers calmly. "We're going to **take them for a ride**."

She doesn't **speed up**. Instead, she makes several right turns until you have driven in a complete circle. The black car continues to follow you.

"Yes, we're definitely being followed," Betty confirms. "The laptops—they must have used them to track us. Damn. Just stay calm. They won't speed up if we don't."

"Do you think we can **outrun** them?" you ask.

"In this van?"

"If only we had a fast car."

Betty smiles. She **whips out** her phone and makes a quick call.

Several minutes later, you are **pulling into** a nearby parking garage. Betty drives the van up to a booth and nods to the parking attendant. He looks in both directions, hands her a set of keys, and lets her proceed through the gate. As she makes a **sharp right turn** onto a ramp, you see the black sports car driving into the garage. "They're **on to us**," you say.

Betty grips the steering wheel until her knuckles turn white. "Our parking attendant friend will delay them at the gate just **long enough** for us to . . . " **Stepping on the gas**, Betty races the van to the top floor of the parking garage and **pulls into** a parking space in the corner.

"Let's go," she says, pointing at the both of you to get out. With her other hand she grabs the shopping bag with the costume.

"We're **ditching our ride**?" you ask.

The three of you **sprint** to the other side of the parking level. She points at another parking spot. Tucked in the space is a silver Porsche with tinted windows. "Time to upgrade the rental."

"Whoa," exclaims Nick. "This job has perks."

Betty unlocks the doors, and the three of you **dive into** the car right before you see the headlights of the black sports car as it drives slowly up the incline. Luckily, it passes right by you because it is looking for the black van. The three of you are silent, not even daring to breathe as the car continues driving around the level, circling like a shark looking for prey. It stops near the black van. The driver **rolls down** the window. You can see him carrying a gun.

"Why don't we just go now?" Nick whispers excitedly.

"Shh," Betty whispers, sinking lower in the driver's seat. "**Get down** and be quiet."

The three of you watch as a man and a woman get out of the car. "Hey, Jules," the man says to the woman. "The van is here, but where'd they go?"

"**Beats me**, Mani. But they can't have gone far." They walk around the van a few times, look under it, and then in all directions. After a few minutes, they look at each other and shrug.

"Do you think we can **pull it off**?" you hear Nick whisper.

If you think that Nick is asking whether you will be able to escape from Foster's spies, go to **page 199**.

If you think that Nick is asking whether you should **drive away** now, go to **page 200**.

Nick is asking whether you will be able to escape from Foster's spies. "Yes, we can **pull it off**," you say. "We'll just **wait them out**."

Nick's question makes you reflect on your mission so far. Before today, if he had asked you the same question, there was no way you would have believed you could accomplish something like this.

"Do you hear that?" Betty **bursts out**.

Go to **page 201**.

Nick is asking whether you should **drive away** now. But at this moment, you don't think it is a good idea to make any sudden moves. Instead, you **duck down** further in your seat.

"Now isn't the right time to **pull away**," you say. "They'll probably notice us in the car, right?"

You see the back of Betty's head nod. "Agreed," she says.

"I know that much, **Sherlock**," Nick says, irritated. "You must think I'm pretty stupid."

You aren't sure why your cousin always accuses you of thinking that you are smarter. Although he doesn't always say the right thing or take situations seriously, he has already proven himself to be a good **sidekick**. You **make a mental note** that once you **get out of this mess**, you will tell him exactly what he means to you. Family should never be **taken for granted**.

"We can **pull this off**—but only if you two stop fighting," Betty exclaims.

"Thank you. That's all I was asking for," Nick explains. "Can we do this?"

Go to **page 199.**

From behind the car, you can hear muffled voices coming closer. Your breathing quickens, and you feel yourself start to sweat. You think that a **showdown** is coming—just like in the finales of all of your crime novels. Betty's eyes glance up at the rearview mirror. You shut your eyes. *This is it.*

"Daddy, I want a T-shirt!" you hear a little girl whine. "Get me a T-shirt that says 'I Heart DC' now!"

"Next time, Madison," the father grumbles. "It's time to go."

Thud, thud. Car doors are opening and closing. Then you hear the car start and begin to **pull away.** You open your eyes and look out the window. Almost at the exact same time, a family of four gets into another car beside you.

Without saying a word, Betty starts the engine of the Porsche. As it **purrs to life**, the car deftly **makes its way** between the other cars that are leaving, unnoticed. The three of you **hold your breath** as you drive down to the street level.

"We did it. We **pulled it off**," Betty says with relief.

Go to **page 202**.

You finally arrive at the National Theater in **good time**—thanks to Betty's speeding in the Porsche. Betty drops you off at the ticket booth to get tickets for the show.

"Three tickets for *CATS*, please," you say to a bald man with thick glasses sitting behind the ticket counter.

The man nods and starts typing into the computer. "Okay, I see here that there are still some seats available. Your total will be $150."

You take out your wallet and start counting your money. But then the man stops typing, stares at his computer screen for a moment and then back at you. "Sir," he says. "Which show did you want?"

"*CATS*," you answer. "It's starting in twenty minutes."

"I need to see some ID first."

"What? Why?"

"Safety precautions, sir. It's a national security **measure** we just **put in place**. This is the capital, after all."

You sigh, **roll your eyes**, and give him your picture ID. He types your information into the computer and frowns. "We just **sold out**."

"You said there were seats available a minute ago!"

"So sorry, sir," he says curtly. But you can tell that he doesn't mean it. His eyes are already looking behind you for the next customer. "Next!"

You move to the side to let other people get their tickets. What should you do now? You have twenty minutes to think of another way to get inside the theater. You observe the ticket seller as he sells tickets to the next customer.

"That's not fair," you protest. Everyone in the line turns to stare at you. "Why don't these people have to show their photo ID?"

"ID checks are random," the man explains. "You got unlucky."

You try to argue your case, but the man just puts his hand up to his ear like he can't hear what you are saying behind the glass window. Now you are furious. You start to walk up to the window to repeat what you said when a police officer grabs your arm.

"Is there a problem, sir?"

You shake you head and walk away. When you find Betty you explain everything. "At first, the man said there were seats available, but then a minute later he said they **sold out**."

"They didn't sell out of tickets," Betty says seriously. "He saw your name. That man **sold us out**. He was **paid off** by someone to not sell the tickets to us. Foster is **behind this**."

"That means he's already here," you say, defeated. "What can we do now? We only have fifteen minutes before the show starts."

Betty and Nick exchange looks and smile. Nick drops the shopping bag at your feet.

"Oh no. You can't be serious," you say when you realize what they are thinking.

"It's the only other way to get into that show," Nick says, trying not to laugh. "And it's the easiest way to get **backstage** where you can find Frida."

"Unfortunately, he's right, David," says Betty.

"**It's show time**," teases Nick.

You carry the bag to the back of the car to change. When you come back dressed in the tight cat costume, Nick has to cover his mouth to keep from laughing. Even Betty can't keep herself from smiling.

"Mr. Meow! You look pretty good as a cat." Nick yanks at your tail, snapping your tights against your legs. "When you go out there, **break a leg**—I mean a tail."

"Very funny," you growl.

"Okay, that's enough, Nick," Betty says, **stepping in**. "David needs to stay focused." She looks at you and points across the street to the theater. "As soon as you find Frida, push the button on your watch. We'll be there."

You nod. You hope this crazy plan works. **Taking a deep breath**, you walk toward the side entrance reserved for the actors and crew. You try to act normal, but the costume's tights **itch like crazy**.

"**Hold on**, sir," a security guard says, stepping forward and blocking your way. "You can't come through here."

"I'm in the show," you insist, pointing at your cat ears. "I'm going to be late."

"**Show's over**," the security guard responds, pushing you back out the door.

If you think that the guard is saying that you are late and that the show has already started, go to **page 205**.

If you think that the guard is saying that he knows you are lying and isn't going to let you in, go to **page 206**.

The guard is saying that you are late and that the show has already started. You look at the time on your smartphone. "But there's still time!" you say. "The show is only supposed to start in ten minutes."

The security guard glares at you as if you are a crazy person. "Don't worry, pal, you'll get your chance to see Dorothy Dixon **in person**. She'll be signing autographs after the show. You'll just have to wait until then."

"You have to believe me," you say more urgently. You stand on your tiptoes and wave your furry paws, trying to **catch the attention** of one of the costumed performers walking by. "Hey! Hey!"

"Okay, I've **had it** with your games, buddy," the guard says, grabbing you roughly by the arm. "You want to keep **putting on a show**? Do it for the cops."

Go to **page 206.**

The guard is saying that he knows you are lying and isn't going to let you in.

"Please, sir," you argue, feeling yourself start to sweat.

"Where's your ID badge then?" he asks, showing you the picture ID he is wearing around his neck. "I don't recognize you, and I've worked here every night."

"I forgot it because I was in a hurry to get here. Isn't it enough that I'm wearing the costume?"

He shakes his head. "Do you know how many crazy **fans** try to get backstage wearing costumes?"

You don't know what to say next. He is right. You have no proof you are in the play. You could just be another one of Dorothy Dixon's adoring fans. You are about to **give up**, when you see someone familiar pass by the door. To your surprise, she stops when she sees you.

"There you are," she says.

The security guard looks at her in surprise. "Do you know this guy, Ms. Dixon?"

"He's one of our **extras**," she answers. "When we did a count earlier, we were missing a person." Then she says to you, "We have to hurry now. The show's about to start."

"I'm sorry about the confusion," the security guard yells after you. "I thought you were just **putting on a show**."

You are so shocked to be face to face with the one person you have been looking for all this time that you say nothing. You just let Frida drag you backstage.

You join a large crowd of other "cats" in various shapes, colors, and sizes. The director is standing on a chair, the only person not in a costume. He nods at Frida. Frida **takes her place** in the front of the group, **striking a pose**. Photographers adjust the lighting and **snap photos**. You take your place beside her and try to pose too, your paws curled in the air. You do your best to follow what the others are doing.

"Before the show starts," you whisper to Frida, "I have to tell you something very important."

She twirls her whiskers nervously. "Not now. **Get back in position!**"

You try another awkward pose and **lean in** closer to Frida. "Do you remember a woman who worked for your family in Houston?"

She shakes her head, but you see a trace of recognition in her eyes.

"Frida, I know you remember Ana," you whisper. "She loved you very much. She **took care of you** when you were **growing up**."

Frida's eyes grow big and she looks around at the other cats to make sure they aren't listening. "**Take five!**" she yells.

"You can't **take a break**, Dorothy," the director says. "You have to be **in position**. The show's about to start."

Frida ignores him and pulls you behind a curtain where you will have more privacy to talk. "Who the hell are you?" she demands.

"I'm Ana's son, David. She's in trouble, Frida. I think your father kidnapped my mother because he thinks she can convince you to come see him. I think he wants a trade."

"What? I can't believe my father **tracked me down**. We stopped talking years ago. I thought that **whole mess** was **behind me**," Frida mutters, shaking her head. "When he went to prison, it ruined our family you know." Her voice cracks. Tears **roll down** her cheeks.

"I know how you feel," you answer quietly. "I also come from a **broken family**. I haven't spoken to my mother in years."

Your confession seems to change Frida's attitude, and she seems more willing listen. "Look," she says, peeking around the curtain. "I'd like to help you. Ana was **like family** to me. And I'd like to see my father again so we can **straighten all this out**. But this isn't the right time—"

"This has to be the right time!" you say sharply. "Foster could kill my mother if you don't talk to him. He could be here right now, waiting in the audience."

She looks away. "What do you want me to do?"

"Call him. Tell him you'll talk to him if he **turns himself in**—if he lets my mother go."

She stares at you for a moment, and then pulls out her cell phone and simply dials his number and waits. "Daddy? Yeah, yeah it's me. I know. Yes, I finally called. Of course. I've always had your number. I just never . . . What? He's here with me." She **looks up** at you. "I know, I know. I'll see you soon. Yes, we need to talk."

You are astonished by how simple it was to find Foster with Frida's help. All it took was a phone call. Suddenly, you feel foolish thinking of your own family situation. *Why didn't I just* **pick up the phone** *and call her during all those years?*

"We're **on our way**," says Frida before **hanging up**. She nods at you as if to say, *it's done.* "He's already left the theater because he doesn't want to meet in public. He wants us to go here." She shows you an address on the phone's screen. "He says no police. Also—" she pauses and shifts her eyes down "—your mother . . . is with him."

"That's great news!"

"Strapped to a bomb."

Your **head spins**. You feel as if you are in a crime novel—and this is the finale. *Guns. Car Chases. Ultimatums. Explosions.*

You knew about the bomb, but you couldn't imagine Foster would be capable of this. You look at Frida. She is your only **bargaining chip**. She is all you have to get back your mother.

"Let's go," you say, grabbing Frida's hand.

Before she goes through the door, she shouts around the curtain to her director and the rest of the *CATS* cast, "There's been a family emergency. But the show **must go on**. Melissa, **you're on!**"

Melissa, who must have been acting in a minor role, looks as if she has won the lottery. "I'm on? I'm on!" She scrambles to the dressing room to change into the lead role costume.

You and Frida **change out** of your costumes, borrow some street clothes from the Art Department, and run to the back of the theater into the alley that leads to the streets.

"Got a car?" she asks you.

Right away, you think of Betty and Nick waiting outside in the front, but then you remember Foster's request not to call the police. If there is one thing you know from your stories, it is that you want to gain a suspect's trust to get him or her to **meet your demands**.

You shake your head. "Let's **hail a cab**."

Just as you **step off** the curb and try to wave at the passing taxis **cruising** the streets, a sports car **pulls up** in front of you. The tinted window **rolls down**. You can only see the green eyes of the driver.

"Get in," Cat says, without looking at you.

It is impossible for you to **read her expression**. Whose **side is she on** now? You left each other on **bad terms** back at Nick's apartment. She even threatened you before she left. But you aren't sure what other choice you have. You just hope she hates Foster more than you right now. You nod at Frida reassuringly, and the two of you **jump in**.

"Before we go, **hand over** your watch," Cat says. "I'm not **taking any chances**."

Ten minutes later, you speed up the ramp of a dimly lit parking garage. Cat continues circling on the parking level until you see a figure emerge. Cat **slams on the breaks**. For a moment, there is silence except for the humming of the car's engine. You find yourself staring at a man with silver hair wearing a dark suit and leather gloves. *This must be the infamous Frederick Foster.* The frightened look on Frida's face tells you that you are right.

"**Look at what the cat dragged in**," Foster calls out in the dark.

If you think that Foster is amused and pleased at how Cat has managed to bring you to him, go to page 210.

If you think that Foster is commenting on how Cat brought you here by force, go to page 212.

Foster is amused and pleased at how Cat has managed to bring you to him. "Nice to see that you're back **on my side**," Foster says to Cat as you both get out of the car.

"I told you I would do this. Now, finish your **end of the bargain**," she replies coldly.

Foster turns on a flashlight and shines it at a dark corner. In the spotlight you see your mother tied up, trembling and sweating against the wall. When she sees you, she starts screaming, trying to say something to you, but the tape over her mouth muffles her cries. There is a complicated system of colorful wires tied around her and sticks of explosives tied to the front of her chest.

Foster speaks to you in a **cold voice**. "I've been trying to get Ana to talk for a week now, but she doesn't want to cooperate."

"**Get to the point**, Foster. Frida is here. What else do you want?"

"What else do I want?" he repeats back, his face slowly **turning red**. At his sides, his hands clench into tight fists. "Thanks to your mother, I was put in prison and I lost my family. I lost my wife and my daughter."

"I brought Frida here for Ana," you say, pointing at your mother. "I convinced your daughter to come. I did everything you wanted. Now, **do your part**."

Frida looks at you and then at her father. Then, in a trembling voice, she manages to say, "I'm here now, Dad. Please let Ana go."

Foster turns to you and points at his daughter. "She's terrified, don't you see? My own daughter thinks I'm a monster. You asked me what else I want? I want Ana to admit she **framed me**. I'm innocent. I've always been innocent. And I want my daughter to know that."

You realize now why Foster is doing all this—the kidnapping, the demands. He wants Ana to **wipe the slate clean** for him. But is it too late for him?

Foster **walks over** to your mother and rips the tape from her mouth. "Tell my daughter, Ana," he demands.

Your mother shakes her head and cowers.

"That's the deal," Foster says, pointing to the explosives on your mother's chest. "You have five minutes **and counting**. **Take it or leave it**."

You watch helplessly as the clock on the bomb's timer **counts down** the seconds. Of course your mother is refusing; she has always done what is right. Telling the truth is the right thing to do. But is she really **willing to die** rather than lie?

Then, from the **corner of your eye**, you see Cat take out a wrinkled, brown paper bag, the kind that might contain a bottle or small container. She looks determined as she steps in front of you. It looks as if Cat is going to **drop a bomb**.

If you think that Cat is going to throw an explosive at Foster, go to **page 213**.

If you think that Cat is going to reveal something dramatic, go to **page 214**.

Foster is commenting on how Cat brought you here by force. Does that mean Cat is working for Foster again? But Cat didn't **drag you here**. You came willingly.

Now you wish you hadn't surrendered your watch to Cat. Here you are in a dark parking garage with a notorious criminal and his agent—and Betty and Nick know nothing about it.

You look at Cat again, trying to **read her**. She looks at Foster with plain disgust. Foster doesn't seem to notice and **wears a smile** that makes you shiver.

Go to **page 210**.

Cat is going to throw an explosive at Foster to end it all. You watch as she reaches into the paper bag. Is it a grenade? A homemade bomb big enough to destroy all of you? **Thinking fast,** you throw yourself in front of your mother, trying to act as a **human shield.**

"Don't do it Cat," you beg. "You don't have to **take it this far.**"

"I have to," Cat says, determined. "It's the right thing to do."

"Don't kill us all!"

Cat looks at you strangely. "Um, no. But I do think it's time that everyone knows the truth."

Go to **page 214.**

Cat is going to reveal something dramatic. "It's time everyone knows the truth about your true intentions, Fred—why you really want to **make amends** with your daughter."

Cat reaches into a brown paper bag and pulls out your watch. Everyone stares at the watch dangling from her fingers and waits for her to continue.

"I've been **doing my homework**, following our hero, David, around for a while, and I've discovered something interesting."

"What are you doing, Cat?" Foster demands, looking panicked.

"Stop acting like the reason we're all here is so that Frida can think her Daddy is a good guy," Cat snaps back at him. She turns away from Foster and looks at the rest of you. "Fred has been **two-timing** me with another one of his she-spies, and I've **had enough**."

"Cat, please," warns Foster. "Don't do this."

Cat looks at him coldly. "What? Reveal what an asshole you are?" She turns to you and your mother. "Fred's daughter is worth a fortune—isn't that right, Ana? Now, for a demonstration . . ."

She twirls around and taps the watch against a cement support column. It isn't a hard strike, but you hear the glass cover break. Cracked open, pieces of the watch fall to the ground. She holds up the watch so that everyone can see the exposed metal gears.

"If I wind the watch like so, everything aligns to reveal something. See?"

You look closer to see what she is talking about. Then you see it. The gears have come together to form a symbol you recognize, a Mayan symbol.

"It means 'home' roughly," Cat announces. "Ingenious, actually."

"**Come on**, Cat," Foster pleads. "**What's done is done**. We can still **split** the money. I deserve that fortune."

"You deserve **life in prison**," Cat says, through clenched teeth. "For betraying your family and everyone who has ever loved you."

She glares at Foster, but you notice her bottom lip begin to quiver. Tears start **rolling down** her cheeks.

Then she does something you don't expect: She pushes the emergency button on the watch.

"They'll be coming for you, Fred," Cat says. "I'm sorry I won't **be around** to see you in handcuffs."

She rips the tracking device out of your watch before putting it on her own wrist. Then she jumps back in her car and **pulls away**. Foster roars in frustration, his voice echoing against the walls of the parking garage. You can tell he doesn't know what to do. Cat has **double-crossed** him, and she is now **on her way** to get the money.

"**It's over**, Foster," you tell him. "Let my mother go. Disable the bomb. It's not too late to **make things right**."

"She's not getting away with this!" he screams.

You think that he is about to lunge at you. Instead, she grabs Frida. She struggles to escape, but he **knocks her out** with a **blow to the head**. He carries her unconscious body into his car. You try to stop him, but he **shoves you off**.

"You can't leave!"

Helpless and terrified, you watch him **take off** with his daughter.

Go to **page 216**.

Now it is just you and your mother. You run to her side and untie her hands. With free hands, your mother helps you untangle the network of wires attached to her.

"Do you have any idea how to stop this?" you ask.

She shakes her head. "They don't teach you this in agent training."

Desperately, you follow the paths of each of the tangled wires with your fingers. There are four different colored wires. Whenever you see this in the movies, the hero has to decide which color wire to cut to **trip the circuit** and prevent the bomb from **going off**. You stare at the ticking timer. It is **down to the last minute**.

"Police!" you hear someone shout from behind you. "Put your hands above your heads where we can see them!"

You **turn around** to see you are surrounded by at least a dozen cops. Betty soon arrives in another car and yells for everyone to lower their guns. "**Hold your fire**! These are not the suspects. The suspects are **on the run**. We have a **possible hostage situation**."

"Help!" you yell. In about thirty seconds, the bomb will explode.

A man in S.W.A.T gear sprints to you and your mother. "**Stand back**. We'll **take it from here**." You read his badge: Lt. Burnside. Three of his men run to your mother and start **poring over** the network of wires. All you can do is watch.

"I think I've seen a setup like this before," one of the men says, pulling out a sharp tool like a pocketknife. "I'm pretty sure we need to cut the blue one. No—wait—the red one." He sticks in his knife and peers closer at the wires. "Yeah, the red one."

"Pretty sure? Are you kidding me?"

"We're S.W.A.T. We don't joke," he **fires back**.

"Okay, okay! Just do it!"

The timer ticks away. *Five, four, three—*

The man cuts the wire. There is a loud beeping sound. You shut your eyes tight and embrace your mother, waiting for the blast.

"Yep, pretty sure," the man says coolly.

A few hours later, dozens of police cars, fire trucks, and ambulances have surrounded the parking garage and the entrances are blocked off with yellow tape to **keep out** curious **bystanders**.

Nick joins you and Betty. He is dazzled by the media attention and stands **in awe** as the news crews interview Betty. Betty stands with the other detectives, **breaking away** from **time to time** to shout orders over the radio. The police are still in **hot pursuit** of Frederick Foster and Catherine Fisher.

The bomb squad and paramedics carefully put your mother on a stretcher and load her into the back of an ambulance. After you hug Nick and Betty goodbye, you climb into the ambulance with your mother. You take her hand and squeeze it.

She opens her eyes. "My son," she whispers. "I—I'm so sorry."

"Don't be sorry. **Comes with the territory**. You were just **doing your job**—as a mother and a detective."

You take the jade ring out of your pocket and slide it on her finger. She smiles like she knows exactly where it came from.

"I never wanted you to **have any part** in this. But when this thing happened with Foster—I knew the only person I could **count on** was you." She stops to **stroke your cheek**.

"I learned from the best. And I learned something else, too: I want to **follow in your footsteps**."

"Are you sure?" your mother says, her eyes wide open now. "You've seen what this job can do."

"With training, it'll be a **piece of cake**," you chuckle. "But only if you and Betty take me **under your wing**. Besides, I think you're going to need some help finding Foster and Cat."

"What about medical school? Aren't you going back home?"

"Nah," you answer. "I am home."

THE END

You decide that you must avoid telling Nick anything. Besides, you have never seen him so happy in his entire life. You just aren't ready to **pull the rug out from under** him and ruin his happiness. You are also worried about making the **wrong move** with Cat.

"Nothing," you answer. You remember Cat's words: "You really think that spy watch can help you? Fred is too smart for Cleaning House, Inc."

After breakfast, Nick gets ready to leave, tossing things into his backpack. You watch him mutely from the couch. Once again, you have doubts about whether **you have what it takes** to help the investigation. Cat might be right. What if this mission is hopeless?

"See you later, Kiddo!" Nick shouts from the front door. He pauses and adds, "And hey, I **believe in** you." He winks at you and walks out of the apartment, whistling to himself.

Go to **page 219**.

Suddenly, your phone rings. The number is blocked. You remember the phone call at Nick's house a few days ago and Cat's stealthy glance at the screen. Betty said no calls, but you are curious.

"Hello?" you answer.

A weak voice comes through. "David? David, is that you?"

"Mother?" you say, shocked.

"Yes!" Then you hear her say to someone in the background, "He answered—he's alive."

"Didn't I tell you?" the person replies.

"David, I thought they had taken you," your mother starts saying. You can hear her **voice crack** with emotion. "They showed me a photo—you looked so frightened."

You recall the **selfie** incident. *So that's why Cat took those photos.* In every shot, you had your hands up, trying to block Cat from taking your picture. You remember how your face looked, how you grimaced as you resisted Cat.

"It looked like you were kidnapped," your mother continues. "I believed it, so I **cracked**. I told them where I hid the money that Foster has been looking for. All that's left is the combination—"

"Look, you can explain everything later. Tell me where you are."

"Wait." You hear her give the phone to someone else.

"Hi, David," says a familiar voice. "I told you we'd be **in touch**."

You aren't too surprised. In fact, you should have expected it. Cat must have **got hold of** your phone number earlier.

"Hello, Cat." You pause for a moment. "Don't hurt my mother."

"Hurt sweet Ana? Of course not," Cat snorts. "I'm not a **monster**, **no matter what** you think."

"You could have fooled me," you say bitterly. "What do you want?"

"Foster wants to meet you. He's at an underground parking garage at a private airport on the outskirts of the city. I'll give you the address in a minute. Listen, Foster knows everything. He knows that the combination to the safe is in your watch."

My watch?

You think about Cat's unusual interest in your watch. It all **makes sense** now. You feel a **pang of regret** for not **acting on** your suspicions sooner. You were rightfully worried about Cat's intentions and yet you did nothing.

"He's willing to **make a trade**," she says.

"My mother for the watch," you guess.

"Well, well. You're **getting the hang of this**. Got a pen?" She gives you the address to the meeting place. "For obvious reasons, don't involve Cleaning House or the police," she warns. "And if you do—"

The phone **goes dead**. She has **made her point**.

You are **in a bind**. You can't tell Betty what is happening. *But maybe I don't have to . . .* With the tracking device in your watch, she should know where you are, though she will probably wonder why you are going to the outskirts of the city. But it is a **delicate situation**. If the authorities get involved, it could **blow the whole deal** and put your mother's life **at risk**. Then again, you have the one thing that Foster wants: your watch.

And yet something still doesn't feel right. Why didn't Cat steal your watch before and take it to Foster herself? Why do *you* need to meet him? From what you know, Foster sounds like he **means business**. You wonder if he has another plan **in mind**.

The drive lasts forty-five minutes. You arrive at a small, private airport **out in the middle of nowhere**. The airport has a runway and several hangars housing small airplanes. At the far side of the runway is a warehouse attached to a parking garage.

You drive your rental car into the garage. It is completely dark so you switch to your **high beams**. Bright lights flood the space. The first level is empty, so you circle around until you find the ramp to a lower, basement level. Now underground, you feel claustrophobic. It is as if the heavy, cement structure is going to fall on top of you. You honk your horn twice and wait. All you can hear is your heart **beating in your chest**.

A moment later, a voice calls out in the darkness. Foster appears in your headlights and **waves you over** to his car, a black limousine that reminds you of a spaceship. Foster himself looks just as you imagined him: trim and handsome, **sporting** silver hair and a pointy mustache.

"Get in, David," he instructs. The passenger door slides open. You join him inside the spacious interior in the back. As the door shuts behind you, you hope that Betty has somehow **figured out** something is wrong and is planning a rescue mission.

"I appreciate that you agreed to meet," Foster says politely, as if this is just a business meeting. "I'll be going **out of the country** for a little while, so it's best we **work things out** now."

For a while, he doesn't say another word. The silence between you is unsettling. Then he **clears his throat** and continues. "You know," he says. "I should kill your mother for all of the pain and suffering she has caused me over these years. She ruined my life."

You nod. "I know you lost everything. In fact, I can understand. I've been separated from my own family for fifteen years. My mother was just trying to do the right thing."

He chuckles at this. "Yes, the right thing. Ana has always been such a **saint**. I don't know about you, but I believe in justice. I **did my time** in prison. I **paid for what I did** and I'm fine with that." He reaches into a seat pocket. "Now it's her turn."

The doors of the limo have been locked. You reach for the door handle but soon realize there isn't one. Foster holds up a remote control and wags his finger at you. He has trapped you inside.

"**Payback**," Foster continues. "Don't you think that's fair?"

If you think that Foster wants revenge, go to page 222.

If you think that Foster just wants the money, go to page 224.

Foster wants revenge, pure and simple. You know now that he has **held a grudge** against your mother all these years. He wants **payback** now—and it has nothing to do with the money. Betty was right about his motive; she just didn't know **how far he was willing to go**. Now you are about to **find out**.

Foster leans toward you, clasping his hands together on his lap. "I'm going to take something very important away from her, just like she did to me."

He pushes a button on his remote control. A door behind you slides open to reveal the trunk section of the limo. At the far end, Cat sits next to your mother. She is holding a gun to her head. When your mother sees you, she looks down at the floor and starts to sob.

"What's happening here?" you demand.

Foster pushes another button. The limo's engine **roars to life**. You are **pulling out** of the parking space.

You look at Cat. A glimmer of doubt appears on her face. She **holds your gaze** for several beats and nods. Without saying a word, Cat grabs your mother, takes out another remote, and unlocks the rear door. Before Foster can react, Cat and your mother both leap out of the moving vehicle.

"David! He's going to—" your mother screams.

The limo's doors are slammed shut again, and you feel the vehicle start accelerating away. Foster is looking away from you, shaking his head and slamming his fist into the roof of the limo, cursing Cat. You try to open the side door, but it is locked again. You throw yourself against the windows, but it is of **no use**. You only hurt your shoulder in the struggle.

When you **turn around** and look out the rear window, you see Cat giving you a long, sad look. She is helping your mother off the ground. You **feel your blood run cold**. Your mother is now sobbing uncontrollably.

As the limo drives away, you wonder where Foster is taking you. Then you see you are turning into an airport where a group of his men are waiting. When the limo doors open, they are prepared. You have no chance of escaping. They move you to one of the airport hangars where you are dragged inside an old propeller-powered airplane. Foster orders one of his men to strap you to the seat—the pilot's seat. The man shuts the door.

The smell of diesel and oil is strong, making you dizzy. Then the plane starts to shudder, shaking violently. From the cockpit window, you see Foster take out another remote control. It looks like one of those controllers for toy airplanes, only bigger. Foster is guiding the plane onto the runway for takeoff—with you inside.

You start pounding your fists against the cockpit window, but it is too late. With another violent shake, you are airborne, rising steadily into the sky. The ascent is too steep, and you are thrown back into the seat. When the plane **levels out**, you see you are about a half mile away from the airport. Washington D.C. is far away over the horizon. Below you are just dusty country roads.

According to the control panel, the plane is now on autopilot. You have no control over the plane, and no way to call for help. As you watch the fuel tank gradually **run out**, you think of one thing—at least your mother is safe.

THE END

Foster just wants the money. You tell him what he wants to hear. "I'm here to **make a deal**. Remember? You want this watch. Right? You get the watch, and you get the money. Let my mother go, and I'll explain to you how the watch works. This watch is useless to you without my help."

You take off the wristband and hold it up to the dim light. It shines temptingly. Foster stares at you blankly. He **drums** his fingers on the leather seat.

"This is your chance to get something back, to **make a life for yourself. Start over** again," you continue.

"Yes, your mother told me about the watch," Foster answers, irritated. "That's why I brought you here. I want my **payback**, all of it—every cent of that fortune. It's mine. And that watch has the code to the safe."

You open the cover of the watch. Then you shake your head. "First, I need **proof of life**. Where's my mother?"

Foster **waves his hand**. "A little **tied up** at the moment but fine."

Suddenly, you see a red beam of light come through the tinted window. It searches the interior of the car, looking for a target. It looks like a search laser.

Betty?

Foster sees the red beam too. Before you realize what is happening, Foster pushes a button on the remote, and the limo's engine start.

"Do you **play me for a fool**?" Foster's face twists with fury. "I said no cops, no Cleaning House. The **deal is off**."

You lunge at Foster and knock him to the floor of the limo. Without thinking, you elbow him in the chest, **knocking the wind out of him**. He releases you as he writhes in pain, dropping his remote control. For a moment, you are **in shock**. You have never been able to **best anyone** in a **face-to-face** fight. Foster sees you looking at the remote and rushes to get it. You reach out and grab his leg, causing him to crash to the floor.

You **climb over** his sprawled body and grab the remote first. You look down at the control panel in your hand. The buttons on the remote are color-coded. You see a green one. Green usually means "go" like on a traffic light. **Taking a gamble**, you press it.

Miraculously, the doors unlock and slide open. You throw yourself out of the vehicle, hitting the concrete hard. You press the emergency button on your watch. *Betty, I hope you're on your way.*

Foster crawls out of the open door. Rather than chase after you, he limps over to the driver's side. He starts the engine manually and slowly brings the car around until its headlights are aimed right at you.

This is it. It looks like Foster is going to ram you with the limo.

Instead, he drives slowly next to you and gives you a cold smile. Another door slides open. A moment later, someone falls out with a dull thud.

"I'm afraid I have to leave, but you should **stay for the show**," Foster says, snickering. "It's **going to be blast**." He gives you a dismissive wave and **drives off**.

The person on the ground groans.

"Are you hurt?" you call out.

"David?" the person answers, confused.

You **break into a run**. Your mother is bound with ropes, trembling and sweating. When she sees you, she starts screaming. She **inches back** away from you.

"It's me, David. I'm here to help," you say to reassure her, but she continues to **back away** from you on the ground. You wonder if she is disoriented and confused about who you really are. She must be **in shock**.

Then you stop **dead in your tracks**. You see it. A metal box with wires is strapped to her chest.

Go to **page 216**.

[GLOSSARY]

THE GLOSSARY DEFINES the phrases and expressions that are tested in the decision points throughout the book.

a storm is coming: an expression used to indicate that something threatening or dangerous is expected

airing dirty laundry: to reveal something that was being kept secret or concealed

boot camp: a challenging training program

butterflies in your stomach: an expression used to describe being nervous or anxious

carried away: to do something impulsive because one got excited or reckless

carry out: to perform or implement some course of action or plan

clean house: to reveal or disclose a conspiracy or crime

come clean: to reveal the truth or to confess a secret or crime

don't leave any stone unturned: to be thorough and careful in one's investigation or inspection

dragging your feet: to be doubtful and unsure

drop a bomb: to reveal a secret or make a confession

everywhere but the kitchen sink: an expression used to describe how someone looked in every possible location or considered every possibility

falling for her: to be enamored with or charmed by someone

following me now: to show trust, to be confident in what a person is saying, to believe a claim made by someone

get away with: to leave or exit from a scene or location; alternatively, to escape or elude responsibility

get your feet wet: to try something for the first time

get under your skin: to bother, disturb, or irritate

give up: to abandon a course of action or plan; alternatively, to reveal some information or to expose someone's plan

go with his gut: to make a decision based on one's feelings or instincts

hang ups: personal conflicts or obsessions with other people; alternatively, to end a phone call abruptly when someone answers the call in order to annoy or intimidate

have a go: to take a chance

hold up: to give support; alternatively, to delay a course of action

in the dark: to be ignorant, to have no knowledge of something

keep an eye on him: to monitor or supervise someone carefully

keep this up: to continue a course of action

let me down: an expression used to show disappointment or regret

letting the cat out of the bag: to divulge or reveal something

make it up to you: to atone and make amends for a personal offense

mixed signals: conflicting actions that lead to a misunderstanding

National Mall: a national memorial park in Washington, D.C.

no place like home: an expression used to emphasize the importance of family and personal history and where one was born or from

payback: revenge; alternatively, some form of restitution

pull it off: to achieve a task or objective with success

rubbing you the wrong way: to annoy or irritate someone

second guessing: to express a lack of confidence in someone

show him the ropes: to train or teach someone

show up: to arrive on the scene, to be present

show us up: to embarrass someone by doing a task better

show's over: an expression used to show that an attempt or effort has failed

showdown: a confrontation or clash between two parties

slipped under the radar: to have escaped detection or notice

sneaks up: to surprise

someone who'd do anything for his mother: an amiable, trustworthy person

sounds like: seems like

stand out: to attract attention, to be different or unusual in some way

straight answer: an honest and sincere response

take matter into your own hands: to act decisively on one's own

the rest is history: an expression used to show that an outcome was to be expected or is obvious

what makes you tick: an inner passion or personal desire

what the cat dragged in: an object or a person that makes a sudden appearance in unusual circumstances

with you now: an expression used to show that one is an ally, friend, or supporter

[ACKNOWLEDGMENTS]

WRITING THIS BOOK has been quite an adventure. First, I would like to express tremendous gratitude to my editors, Karen Hannah and Genevieve DeGuzman, for believing in me as a writer and teaching me how to make a story come alive. They have succeeded in turning a novel idea into a series of books that enables ESL students to interact with the text and learn language in more engaging, meaningful ways.

I want to thank my mother, Cindy, and my grandmother, Nanny, who have cultivated my love for reading and believed in me as an author since I was just a little girl writing in cloth journals and on the backs of pantyhose packages. I would also like to thank all of my family members and friends in my hometown of Lebanon, Pennsylvania, as well as my new friends and colleagues in my adopted town of Washington, D.C., who were my support system during the entire writing process. Specifically, I want to thank Jesica Thavarajah, Julie Seiwell, Hector Machorro, and Mani Parcham for being my sounding board and providing inspiration for some of the more colorful characters and events that occur in the book.

Finally, I would like to recognize all of my former students from Roosevelt High School and all of my current and former students at Williamsburg Middle School for inspiring me in the classroom. They have not only taught me how to be a better teacher but also have inspired me to write stories about their diverse experiences.

REBECCA M. KARLI lives in Washington, D.C. and works as a middle school ESL teacher in Arlington, VA. Writing stories on an old typewriter and on the back of restaurant placemats since the age of 7, Rebecca has dreamed of becoming an author all her life. Now, her dream is to write and publish literature that is relevant, engaging, and speaks to the diverse experiences of her ESL students. In addition to teaching and writing, Rebecca enjoys learning new languages, traveling to different countries, and following current events. She also loves spending time with her friends and family, and being amused by her cat, Frida Kitty Kahlo.

[ABOUT THE PUBLISHER]

NIGHT OWLS PRESS (nightowlspress.com) is a small, independent press that publishes nonfiction books that challenge and re-imagine prevailing conventions about business, work, and life. Covering topics on entrepreneurship, education, innovation, and social responsibility, its focus is to turn big ideas into great books that inform and inspire.

Find out more about Night Owls Press books at www.nightowlspress.com/e-book-store/. For special orders and bulk purchases, contact admin@nightowlspress.com.

[ABOUT THE SERIES]

TURN OF PHRASE ESL (TOP ESL) is the first-ever educational series that introduces English language learners to idioms, phrasal verbs, and collocations in the form of chooseable path novels. TOP ESL is designed for intermediate to advanced level young adult and adult learners.

Find out more about the series at www.nightowlspress.com/turn-of-phrase-esl/ or visit www.nightowlspress.com/e-book-store/ and search for TOP ESL titles. For orders or to request a series catalog, contact admin@nightowlspress.com.

Available titles:

> *An Artful Heist* by Jacob Jun
> *Blackout* by G.K. Gilbert
> *Cleaning House* by Rebecca M. Karli
> *The Spoonmaker's Diamond* by Mary M. Slechta